Scarecrow Studies in Young Adult Literature
Series Editor: Patty Campbell

Scarecrow Studies in Young Adult Literature is intended to continue the body of critical writing established in Twayne's Young Adult Authors Series and to expand it beyond single-author studies to explorations of genres, multicultural writing, and controversial issues in YA reading. Many of the contributing authors of the series are among the leading scholars and critics of adolescent literature, and some are even YA novelists themselves.

The series is shaped by its editor, Patty Campbell, who is a renowned authority in the field, with a twenty-eight-year background as critic, lecturer, librarian, and teacher of young adult literature. In 1989 she was the winner of the American Library Association's Grolier Award for distinguished service to young adults and reading.

1. *What's So Scary about R.L. Stine?* by Patrick Jones, 1998.
2. *Ann Rinaldi: Historian and Storyteller,* by Jeanne M. McGlinn, 2000.
3. *Norma Fox Mazer: A Writer's World,* by Arthea J. S. Reed, 2000.
4. *Exploding the Myths: The Truth about Teenagers and Reading*, by Marc Aronson, 2001.
5. *The Agony and the Eggplant: Daniel Pinkwater's Heroic Struggles in the Name of YA Literature*, by Walter Hogan, 2001.

The Agony and the Eggplant

Daniel Pinkwater's Heroic Struggles in the Name of YA Literature

Walter Hogan

Scarecrow Studies in Young Adult Literature, No. 5

The Scarecrow Press, Inc.
Lanham, Maryland, and London
2001

SCARECROW PRESS, INC.

Published in the United States of America
by Scarecrow Press, Inc.
4720 Boston Way, Lanham, Maryland 20706
www.scarecrowpress.com

4 Pleydell Gardens, Folkestone
Kent CT20 2DN, England

Copyright © 2001 by Walter Hogan

British Library Cataloguing-in-Publication Information Available

Library of Congress Cataloging-in-Publication Data
Hogan, Walter, 1949–
   The agony and the eggplant : Daniel Pinkwater's heroic struggles in the name of YA literature / Walter Hogan.
      p. cm. — (Scarecrow studies in young adult literature ; no. 5)
   Includes bibliographical references and index.
   ISBN 0-8108-3994-6 (alk. paper)
   1. Pinkwater, Daniel Manus, 1941—Criticism and interpretation. 2. Young adult fiction, American—History and criticism. I. Title. II. Scarecrow studies in young adult literature ; 5.
PS3566.I526 Z69 2001
813'.54—dc21   00-067047

♾™ The paper used in this publication meets the minimum requirements of American National Standard for Information Sciences—Permanence of Paper for Printed Library Materials, ANSI/NISO Z39.48–1992.
Manufactured in the United States of America.

To Jeremy,
who many years ago brought home
a book with the curious title,
Yobgorgle, Mystery Monster of Lake Ontario,
and asked me to read it to him

Contents

Acknowledgments

I first wish to thank Daniel Pinkwater for his generosity in patiently answering my numerous questions about his work. Our communication was primarily by email, over a period of about nine months from the time this manuscript was conceived until, after much labor, it was finally delivered to my wonderful editor, Patty Campbell. Those fecund responses from the Master himself are perhaps the best passages in this book, whose title and subtitle must also be credited to Mr. Pinkwater. He may have been surprised that we actually used a title suggestion that he probably meant as a joke. Perhaps he should have heeded the wise proverb: one man's baby may be another man's eggplant. Or one man's eggplant may be another man's agony. Or his avocado. Or something like that.

I would also like to thank my eighth grade teacher, Sister Mary David, affectionately known as "The Beaver," who used to tell us, "Every dog has his day and every cat has two afternoons."

Finally, I want to thank the University of Michigan for providing me the excellent liberal arts education which equipped me with all the big words I have scattered nonchalantly throughout this learned disquisition, and Eastern Michigan University for being, seriously, a great place to work.

Permission to quote from email correspondence between D. Pinkwater and W. Hogan granted by Daniel Pinkwater.

Permission to quote from *Hoboken Fish and Chicago Whistle* (Princeton, N.J.: XLibris, 1999) granted by Daniel Pinkwater.

Permission to quote from material posted by Daniel Pinkwater to *The (Sort of) Official Daniel Pinkwater Website* <http://www.designfoundry.com/p-zone/> graciously granted by Mr. Pinkwater. That site has since been renamed *The P-Zone: Aileron's Unofficial Pinkwater Website* and relocated to <http://pinkwater.com/pzone/>.

See also *The Official Pinkwater Page* <http://www.pinkwater.com>.

Chronology

1941 Daniel Manus Pinkwater born 15 November in Memphis, Tennessee.
1943 Family relocates to Chicago.
1950 Family moves to Los Angeles.
1955 Family returns to Chicago.
1959 Enrolls in Bard College, New York.
1964 Graduates from Bard with B. A. in Art.
1965 Completes sculpture apprenticeship with David Nyvall. Rents studio loft in Hoboken, New Jersey to begin career as artist. Teaches art and art therapy at several institutions in the New York City area.
1967 Travels around the world, visiting Africa and Japan.
1969 Marries Jill Miriam Schutz, 12 October.
1970 Publishes first book: *The Terrible Roar*
1975 *Wingman* (First intermediate book.)
1976 *Lizard Music* (First novel, receives ALA Notable Book award.)
1977 *Fat Men From Space*
        The Hoboken Chicken Emergency
1978 *The Last Guru*
1979 *Alan Mendelsohn, the Boy from Mars*
        Yobgorgle, Mystery Monster of Lake Ontario
1980 Moves to Hyde Park, New York, in the Hudson Valley.
        The Magic Moscow
1981 *Attila the Pun*
        The Worms of Kukumlima
1982 *Slaves of Spiegel*
        The Snarkout Boys and the Avocado of Death
        Young Adult Novel
1984 *The Snarkout Boys and the Baconburg Horror*
1985 *Young Adults*
1986 Begins decade-long stint as a regular commentator, National Public Radio's "All Things Considered."
1990 *Borgel*
1996 Begins broadcasting reviews of children's books on NPR's *Weekend Edition Saturday* with Scott Simon.

Chapter 1

The Life of the Master

Daniel Pinkwater tells us that his family was not especially prosperous at the time of his birth on November 15, 1941. The author recounts a family story in which he appeared in the living room, a toddler not yet two years old, "holding by the tails a brace of dead Norway rats, one in each hand. I must have taken them out of traps in the kitchen. We had plenty of rats and not a great deal else."[1] His father was born in Poland shortly before the turn of the century, and emigrated to the United States as a young man, soon after the First World War ended in late 1918. He "arrived in New York with a little more than two dollars in his pocket," and migrated across the country, working at a variety of odd jobs.

One standard reference work describes Pinkwater as the "son of Philip (a ragman) and Fay (a chorus girl); maiden name, Hoffman." The directory entry continues, "Politics: 'Taoist.' Religion: 'Republican.'"[2] We might mention at this point that most of the biographical information about Pinkwater—in the directory entry above, in the present book, indeed in every published source—has been provided by the author himself. It is more certain to entertain than to inform.

Sometimes Pinkwater attributes the unresolved mysteries about his origins to other family members. He once told a Welsh correspondent, "My mother claimed to have been born in Cardiff, Wales—but she was notably unreliable. I was there once, and didn't see anybody I recognized. Unless, of course, I have the wrong town in mind. Cardiff is on the sea, and has a big castle, right?"[3]

When asked if his mother were still alive, and if she had ever worked outside the home, Pinkwater replied, "Mother not living. Was a gun-moll during the 1920s."[4] Pinkwater had two half brothers and two half sisters, some of whom are briefly mentioned in his autobiographical essays and in some of his interviews.

When Daniel was about two years old, the family relocated from Memphis, Tennessee to Chicago, "to a big apartment, without rats, a half-block from Lake Shore Drive." There they resided for about six years.

I've often wondered who and what I might have become had I grown up living there, had I gone through elementary school and high school living in one place, knowing the same people, the same streets.

But it wasn't like that for me, or the rest of my family. My father liked to move about. By the time I was ready for college, we had changed domiciles thirteen times, swapped cities six times, and I had attended ten schools.[5]

The Pinkwaters returned to Chicago in the mid-1950s, having spent much of the previous six years in Los Angeles. Pinkwater's feelings about Los Angeles may be inferred from by the insistence of some of his fictional characters that Los Angeles does not exist.[6] Pinkwater describes the city as being "famous for its relative featurelessness, its dearth of public transport, and prohibitive pedestrian distances between points."[7] Daniel was happy to return to Chicago. However, like his character Leonard Neeble in *Alan Mendelsohn, the Boy from Mars*, Pinkwater had to cope with both a new school and a new neighborhood in which he had no friends.[8]

Pinkwater tells us that, like his fictional characters Leonard Neeble and Robert Nifkin, he sometimes rode a city bus downtown after school, or instead of going to school. Like Robert Nifkin, the Snarkout boys, and many of his other characters, Pinkwater sought out both cultural and popular urban entertainment, and he enjoyed the sights and the journeys themselves as much as the destinations. "I began my practice of urban tourism, which continues to this day. I wandered everywhere, walking for hours—took buses to the end of the line, just to see where they would go—prowled around strange neighborhoods—and studied maps of the city."[9] His destinations included those serving food: "It was about this time that I began an earnest pursuit of the other activity which has characterized and shaped my life—gluttony. My funds were limited, but I was able to sample many truly frightening varieties of 1950s junk food."[10]

Pinkwater's father possessed a great deal of entrepreneurial energy,[11] and by the time Daniel graduated from high school, the family had attained a level of prosperity sufficient to finance Daniel's matriculation at a private college. As Pinkwater tells it, "I defied the predictions of guidance counselors and juvenile officers and left for college."[12]

Putting some distance between himself and a domineering father must have been a liberating experience.

I liked being at college. For one thing it meant I was not at home, working for him. My brothers worked for him. They had nervous tics, and were given to staring into space with doomed expressions. Going to work for my father was something like being in the French Foreign Legion or the Turkish navy, only not as much fun.[13]

Pinkwater clearly respected his father and admired some of his qualities. He tells many lively stories about Pinkwater senior, and in one interview he said that his father "was from the old country, and was like one of Isaac Babel's father characters—just the kind of father a boy wants to have. . . . I loved my father. He toughened me."[14] However, in another interview, Pinkwater had this to say about his upbringing:

I come from a highly dysfunctional family.[15] Fortunately, I had an elder half-brother and half-sister, whom my mother had at one time parked in an orphanage for a few years because that was convenient. They acquired human values there, and they raised me. But my actual biological parents were straight out of the Pleistocene. My father dealt out what could be called the discipline. It was actually just abuse. He would vacillate between scaring me and shouting at me and whacking my knuckles with the handle of a knife because I was a fat elephant.[16]

All in all, Pinkwater père seems to have been the type of father with whom a child could only have a love-hate relationship.

Daniel journeyed from the Midwest to attend Bard College, in New York's Hudson Valley, not far from where the author resides today.

The . . . college I went to is about the most beautifully situated place I've ever seen. Coming from Chicago, and hardly ever having been in the country, let alone the hills and mountains and forests of the Hudson River valley in upstate New York, I was continually astonished and distracted by scenery.[17]

At Bard, Pinkwater had numerous experiences he later memorialized in essays and in fiction, including the settling of a score with an oafish lout much like the infamous John Holyrood, "The Beast of Nixonn Hall," whose unspeakable behavior is chronicled in *Dada Boys in Collitch*.[18] Pinkwater earned a B. A. in Art in 1964, after several changes of major. His decision to concentrate upon art is described in an essay in which his father suddenly appeared unannounced at the young Pinkwater's dormitory room, following a thousand-mile journey, demanding that Daniel concentrate upon a single subject—any subject—if he wished to remain at college. Pinkwater goes on, "I don't know why I said art. Until that moment I hadn't considered it seriously."[19] Elsewhere, though, Pinkwater has said that he studied sculpture in order to learn how to become a writer, particularly to learn about form.[20]

As a child and teenager, Pinkwater had dabbled with the visual arts, and in his essays he recalls early trials with drawing and sculpture. He suspects he was attracted to three-dimensional art because of his appreciation for urban architecture. "Friends and family predicted that young Pinkwater would become a writer, however. 'I always told a lot of jokes and made up funny stories: that's where they all got the idea.'"[21]

In his hilarious contribution to the *Something About the Author Autobiography Series*, Pinkwater relates several anecdotes about crucial childhood experiences that influenced his eventual career choices:

> Of my early life I remember many hardships and privations, the worst of which consisted of tripping over a root in Lincoln Park, in Chicago, and scraping my knee on a sharp rock. I remember my sister putting iodine and two band-aids on the wound. It hurt a lot.
>
> I believe that my resolve to become some sort of artist began during the period of recuperation from that injury. I decided that I wanted to work indoors.[22]

Pinkwater goes on to relate that shortly afterwards, he cut himself while carving with a Junior Sculptor's kit. "Gravely disappointed by this second painful experience," young Daniel then gave up sculpture for a number of years.[23]

The possibility of his becoming a writer rather than an artist was to remain an open question for some time. During school holidays from college, and for some time after his graduation, Pinkwater apprenticed with the sculptor David Nyvall. Pinkwater recounts this experience in several of the essays collected in *Hoboken Fish*. At the end of the apprenticeship, Nyvall told Pinkwater that he expected him to become a writer, not a sculptor. "A writer! I don't want to be a writer! Everybody tells me I'm going to be a writer! Writers are sissies! They sit around, bending over typewriters, polluting the atmosphere with unnecessary words. They get eyestrain and backache and coffee nerves and typist's elbow."[24] Pinkwater added in an interview, "I had forgotten that I ever wanted to be a writer. My teacher insisted that I was going to be a writer. He was a pretty smart guy, but I resisted for four more years."[25]

Those next several years were eventful ones for Pinkwater. He rented a studio loft in Hoboken, New Jersey, directly across the Hudson River from New York City. While trying to crack the highly competitive New York artists' scene, he taught art and art therapy at several settlement houses[26] in the region. Pinkwater became deeply involved with children's art, and took an intensive course in art therapy to enhance his teaching credentials.[27] At the same time, he was beginning to achieve success as an artist himself. A Manhattan couple became dedicated collectors of his prints and sculptural works. One of his large woodcut prints was selected for inclusion in the prestigious Brooklyn Museum Biennial exhibit. The prospect of a career as an artist finally seemed attainable.

At about the same time, Pinkwater had also gotten his foot into the door of the world of children's book publishing. By chance, at a party he met an editor who was looking for modern African illustrations. Having just returned from Tanzania,[28] he was able to show her some of his African-inspired work, and she suggested he try illustrating a story. According to Pinkwater, "I had to get a story first, and not wishing to deal with writers, because I knew what *they* were like, I wrote one."[29] That book was *The Terrible Roar* (1970), the first of many children's books to be written and illustrated by Pinkwater. *The Terrible Roar* has been praised for "the sophisticated simplicity and wit of [its] graphic design."[30] Pinkwater remembers, "Working on the drawings—and even more, the writing—was intensely pleasurable."[31]

As with many of the events of his life, Pinkwater has offered us several different versions of the story behind his becoming a children's author. An especially poignant account:

> Half-alive, half-starved, and more than half-crazy, I wandered the streets of New York for weeks on end. At this very point, when all seemed darkest, a passing children's book editor offered me a standard contract for a picture book. Long since having lost every vestige of self-respect, I accepted the terms offered, and with a ballpoint pen stolen from a post office I undertook my first work as an author and illustrator. I knew at once that I had found my calling.[32]

Pinkwater married Jill Miriam Schutz on October 12, 1969. Jill, a native of the Bronx and the daughter of a painter,[33] has since become a successful author and illustrator in her own right. (According to Pinkwater, she had previously been "a noted sportswoman and daredevil . . . a member of the American Busz-Kashi team, [and] had just broken the world record for women's toad-thumping.")[34] By this time, Jill was teaching at a university, and Pinkwater was working as an art instructor at a residential treatment center for boys. As he puts it, he was "moving away from the front lines of mental health care and toward a life of literary art and domesticity. I got married and quit my job, in that order."[35]

With the benefit of hindsight, it now seems logical that Pinkwater would gravitate away from salaried positions and become fully self-employed. He possesses many of the qualities that characterize those who work for themselves. From his father, he inherited toughness, entrepreneurial skills, and the courage to go his own way and take risks. A nonconformist, self-reliant, and a highly creative thinker, it is difficult to envision Pinkwater in any subordinate position. His denunciations of small-minded and pompous bureaucrats of the educational and publishing establishments, in both his fiction and in his autobiographical essays, bespeak an independent outlook and an intolerance of dullards and fools.

So perhaps it was inevitable that Pinkwater would become a creative artist of some sort. But which would it be: the visual arts or literature? Pinkwater told an interviewer,

> For the first few books, I was more interested in creating vehicles for illustration. . . . I had no particular ambitions to continue. "I'm going to stop doing art, and be a writer," was never one of my thoughts. I was still teaching art, eking out a living, being a beatnik. The children's books were just another job. Then the stories became more interesting to me, and I began to come to grips with what my teacher had told me.[36]

In his autobiographical memoirs, Pinkwater also tells of a growing disillusionment with the creation of art works for adult audiences. In one essay, he tells of working on woodcuts in his studio as a college senior on the day that President Kennedy was assassinated, November 22, 1963. Reviewing all of the crises of that time—Vietnam, Cuban missiles, the Berlin Wall, racial tensions—and now the assassination, Pinkwater concluded, "And I was learning to do what? I was learning to make things for rich people to decorate their apartments with. I felt useless and stupid."[37] Although the story ends with an affirmation of the value of art, such thoughts in the head of a student who had just celebrated his twenty-second birthday a week before the assassination evince a genuine desire to make a social contribution while earning his living.

That Pinkwater has enriched the lives of many people is evident from his voluminous correspondence with his readers and radio listeners. Upon receiving a photo of a family of his fans posing with their pet turkey, Goonda, he commented, "This is why I am so happy. . . . It's next to impossible to get rich writing children's books, but if you do a good job, you receive the goodwill of many fine Americans . . . and their children . . . and their turkeys."[38] Joking aside, Pinkwater clearly derives enormous satisfaction from the warm reception of his works by a diverse and enthusiastic audience. As noted in the "About the Author" statement at the end of *Hoboken Fish*, "He receives thousands of letters yearly, written in crayon—some of them from children."[39] On the whole, he prefers the children's letters: "They're a big part of the payoff for being a kids' author. These kids are great!" Whereas adults, he says, too often "write to make statements, kids write to ask questions. This, in a nutshell, is why I prefer writing for kids."[40]

Pinkwater tells another story about his shift from the visual to the verbal arts. When his woodcut print was installed in the prestigious Brooklyn Museum exhibit, "between a Jasper Johns and a Carol Summers," Pinkwater hung around the gallery to eavesdrop on the reactions of the art-lovers. He was disappointed. "The kids in my classes pay better attention to what they're looking at than these museum cooties," he reflected. Then he realized that all the time during which he had been considering a design for another current project—a large outdoor wall mural—"I'd been thinking of it in terms of what somebody maybe eight years old would see on his way to school. I'd identified my audience."[41]

And so Daniel Pinkwater became an author and illustrator of children's books. Until recently, he illustrated nearly all of the books himself. However, since 1996 the artwork for his stories has been taken over by his wife. Thus Pinkwater has finally completed the conversion from artist to writer. Although his drawings have delighted many readers, giving up the task may be a relief to the author. He once said, "I have no problem with the writing. Where I draw breath and get dry in the mouth is when I have to draw pictures, because I know about that. I even have a degree. I suffer from self consciousness, and even though I'm opposed to that kind of thinking, it's hard to escape."[42] Pinkwater recently replied to an email question about his future art work: "I have no plans to do any drawing at all any more, now that Jill has started to illustrate. Isn't she great? She draws like I would if I could really draw."[43]

As he began writing and illustrating stories for children, Pinkwater started with short picture books, and gradually began taking on longer formats as well. His first four publications were slender picture books. The next two, *Fat Elliot and the Gorilla* (1974) and *Wingman* (1975) were also illustrated, but contain considerably more text. While continuing to produce picture books, Pinkwater began writing full-length novels for young readers, beginning with *Lizard Music* in 1976. That novel, illustrated with Pinkwater's wood or linoleum cuts, still remains one of his best-known and most beloved books. During the next decade, Pinkwater's output of novels and illustrated stories exceeded his publication of picture books. Between 1976 and 1985, Pinkwater issued numerous titles in each category of children's books: short picture books for very young children, longer picture books, intermediate stories with and without illustrations, and young adult novels for adolescents. Pinkwater's first young adult novel, *Alan Mendelsohn, the Boy from Mars*, appeared in 1979. It was followed by three more young adult novels during the next five years: *The Snarkout Boys and the Avocado of Death* (1982), *Young Adult Novel* (1982), and *The Snarkout Boys and the Baconburg Horror* (1984). *Young Adults*, a book containing sequels to *Young Adult Novel*, was published in 1985, rounding out this period during which most of Pinkwater's longer fictional works were written.

Since the mid-1980s, Pinkwater has continued, and even accelerated his steady output of picture books, as we shall document in the next chapter. However, his publication of longer fiction has decreased during the past fifteen years. As he explained recently in response to an emailed question, this has been due to the interests of his publishers, and not necessarily to his own inclinations: "I don't know what I may write in the future. It depends a lot on what publishers are willing to buy, (in case anyone has wondered why there has only been one kid's novel since 1988)."[44]

After residing in Hoboken for a number of years, the Pinkwaters moved to Long Island in 1977 and then to their current residence in a two-hundred-year-old farmhouse in Hyde Park, New York, in 1980. Both Pinkwaters are great animal lovers, and their relocation to the countryside has afforded them space to maintain a menagerie including horses and large dogs. (There have been rumors, and even dust jacket photographs of a small herd of rhinos on the farm, but we have been unable to verify these observations due to the elusiveness of the nimble beasts.)[45] The Pinkwaters ran a dog-training business in the 1970s, and they co-authored a well-received book on the subject.[46] Several of Pinkwater's fictional works are dedicated to his favorite canine and feline companions, and many of his best autobiographical essays concern animals he has known. The influence of a lifetime of close relationships with companion animals upon Pinkwater's fiction is immediately evident to readers.

The Pinkwaters do not have children, and when asked how this has affected his work as a writer and illustrator of children's books, Pinkwater responded, "Having them would make it easier, if they could type, and correct my spelling, and get the mail and take phone messages. But I struggle along without such assistance."[47]

The gift for verbal humor which led his friends and family members to suggest that he might become a writer eventually led Pinkwater to a career as a radio personality. After some fourteen years on the airwaves of National Public Radio, Pinkwater is by now as well known for his broadcasts as for his books. Many adults who have enjoyed Pinkwater's radio commentaries have had no exposure to the storyteller's books for children.

Pinkwater has graced the airwaves of several NPR venues. In 1987, he began sending in taped commentaries, usually about three minutes in length, to NPR's *All Things Considered*, and joined that colorful group of NPR raconteurs whose members have included Baxter Black, Andrei Codrescu, and Bailey White (the latter became a commentator through her correspondence with Pinkwater.)[48] Commentaries from the first two years of Pinkwater's taped broadcasts were collected in *Fish Whistle*, and from the next two years in *Hoboken Days and Chicago Nights*, both reprinted together, along with several essays Pinkwater had previously published in various periodicals, as *Hoboken Fish and Chicago Whistle*.

In 1996, Pinkwater began discussing children's books with NPR's *Weekend Edition Saturday* host Scott Simon. Roughly one Saturday per month, Pinkwater and Simon read from and discuss some new children's books on the program. Exposure on the Saturday morning program, heard by 2.3 million listeners, has had an enormous positive impact upon sales of the books mentioned. One publicity director for a major book company called Pinkwater the "Oprah" of the children's corner of the book world.[49] A *Publisher's Weekly* article documented the "impressive, immediate effect on sales" of Pinkwater's reviews, as in the following example of a book by Fred Marcellino reviewed in late 1999: "At 10:00 a.m. on November 13, when the NPR segment was just airing, *I, Crocodile* was number 13,332 in Amazon.com's sales rankings; by 11:15 a.m., the book had jumped to 229. And by midnight, it had reached its highest point, at 24."[50] Immediate, indeed! One can almost hear the simultaneous clicking of thousands of mice in homes across the nation as parents with credit cards responded to that review.[51]

Pinkwater is also a frequent guest caller on the popular NPR program *Car Talk*, where he converses knowledgeably with the Tappet brothers about such esoteric subjects as canine mobile eructation (dogs vomiting in cars), and the width of various car seats relative to the posterior of a "circumferentially challenged" person such as himself.[52]

In 1998, Pinkwater developed a new weekly radio program for children and for adults interested in children's literature. *Chinwag Theater* began in Iowa, where producer Charity Nebbe was based at that time, and has recently moved to Michigan Radio. Now heard on a growing number of public radio stations, the half-hour program features music, banter between Daniel and Charity, and readings from children's books, including Pinkwater's own works. The author noted,

> Some of my works are now out of print and extremely hard to find, so this is giving me a digital archive of my work. And to tell you the truth, I enjoy it. It's fun. I feel very comfortable sitting all alone in a room in my house talking into a receiver. It may be what I do best.[53]

Unquestionably, Daniel Pinkwater is a terrific radio commentator. His rich, pleasant baritone voice is complemented by beautifully precise enunciation. His remarks are witty and entertaining—or emotionally moving, depending upon the topic—and his timing and delivery exquisite. Hearing him read his own stories on the radio is a treat. The absence of illustrations is more than compensated by the excellence of his oral presentation. It may be, as Pinkwater says, that oral storytelling is what he does best, but when he reads from his own books, he's working with some pretty good material. Let's take a closer look at the children's fiction written and illustrated by this multi-talented artist.

NOTES

1. Daniel Pinkwater, *Hoboken Fish and Chicago Whistle* (Princeton, N.J.: Xlibris, 1999), 241.
2. *Contemporary Authors* (Detroit: Gale Research, 1978), vols. 29-32, First Revision, 529. In the same vein, Pinkwater once responded to a fan that his favorite ice cream is "split pea" and his favorite cartoon show "the NBC Evening News." *The (Sort of) Official Daniel Pinkwater Website, Talk to DP Forum* <http://www.designfoundry.com/p-zone> (12 May 2000).
3. Pinkwater's response to an email question posted on the *Talk to DP Forum, Archive*, 27 (8 March 2000).
4. Email from D. Pinkwater to W. Hogan, 16 May 2000.
5. *Hoboken Fish*, 242.
6. This is a running gag in *The Worms of Kukumlima*.
7. *Hoboken Fish*, 243.

8. Some of the events of *Alan Mendelsohn*, particularly Alan's claim to be a Martian, were based upon the author's experiences in junior high school in Los Angeles. (*Hoboken Fish*, 345.)

9. *Hoboken Fish*, 243.

10. *Hoboken Fish*, 23.

11. Seamus Finneganstein, owner and founder of the World Famous Salami Snap Company in *The Worms of Kukumlima*, displays a talent for making money through odd inventions and business deals that parallels the schemes of Pinkwater's father as described in several of the autobiographical essays in *Hoboken Fish*.

12. *Hoboken Fish*, 25.

13. *Hoboken Fish*, 257.

14. *Authors and Artists for Young Adults* (Detroit: Gale Research), vol. 1, 232.

15. A fan who had read this interview in *FAT!SO?* emailed Pinkwater that he was fined 10 cents for saying "dysfunctional" in the interview (per a practice of the Dada Ducks in *Young Adult Novel*.) Pinkwater replied, "Things in interviews are the responsibility of the interviewer/editor. I know. I've been interviewed plenty. Assume 50% of what's there is wrong. So I can deny saying dysfunctional. Ha." *Talk to DP Forum, Archive*, 23 (28 May 2000). The serious point here is that comments attributed to Pinkwater in published interviews should be taken with a grain of salt; they may have been selectively edited and taken out of context. Or Pinkwater's intent may have been to entertain rather than to provide accurate information.

16. Marilyn Wann, "Daniel Pinkwater and the Afterlife." *FAT!SO?* <http://www.fatso.com/interview.html> (11 May 2000).

17. *Hoboken Fish*, 90.

18. *Dada Boys in Collitch* is one of the stories in *Young Adults* (New York: Tom Doherty Associates, 1985). Sadly, *Young Adults* is currently out of print.

19. *Hoboken Fish*, 258.

20. *Something About the Author* (Detroit: Gale Research, 1987), vol. 46, 180.

21. *Junior Literary Guild*, Sept. 1977, quoted in *Authors and Artists for Young Adults*, 233.

22. *Something About the Author Autobiography Series* (Detroit: Gale Research, 1987), vol. 3, 223.

23. *Something About the Author Autobiography Series*, vol. 3, 223.

24. *Hoboken Fish*, 280.

25. *Something About the Author*, vol. 46, 181.

26. A settlement house is "a welfare center providing community services in an underprivileged area." *Illustrated Heritage Dictionary and Information Book* (Boston: Houghton-Mifflin, 1977)

27. *Hoboken Fish*, 337.

28. Pinkwater traveled around the world during 1967-1968, stopping for lengthy visits in Africa and Japan. However, since then his travels have been less exotic; he notes that his last journey aboard an airplane took place in 1970. (*Hoboken Fish*, 204.)

29. *Something About the Author*, vol. 46, 182.

30. *Twentieth-Century Children's Writers*, 3rd ed. (Chicago: St. James Press, 1989), 782.

31. *Hoboken Fish*, 338.

32. *Something About the Author Autobiography Series*, vol. 3, 224.

33. "Her mother was the painter. Her father was an enthusiastic amateur tango dancer." Email from D. Pinkwater to W. Hogan, 16 May 2000.

34. *Something About the Author Autobiography Series*, vol. 3, 225.

35. *Hoboken Fish*, 117.

36. *Authors and Artists for Young Adults*, vol. 1, 234.

37. *Hoboken Fish*, 270.

38. *Hoboken Fish*, 361.

39. *Hoboken Fish*, 395.

40. *Hoboken Fish*, 173.

41. *Hoboken Fish*, 338.

42. *Authors and Artists for Young Adults*, vol. 1, 239.

43. Pinkwater's response to an email question posted on the *Talk to DP Forum* during 1998 (10 September 1999).

44. *Talk to DP Forum,* (14 January 2000).

45. When a fan writing to the Pinkwater Website raised the possibility of dropping in, Pinkwater mentioned some other interesting denizens of his farm: "You'd be welcome to visit, but there's the consideration of insurance, and the rottweilers, and the attack-chimps, and the man-traps, and the specially-trained fungi. Best to stick to the internet posts." *Talk to DP Forum, Archive*, 22 (21 May 2000).

46. Daniel and Jill Pinkwater, *Superpuppy: How to Choose, Raise, and Train the Best Possible Dog For You* (New York: Clarion, 1976).

47. Doug Blackburn, "*All Things Considered* Personality Charms Airwaves, Kids' Imaginations." (Albany) *Times Union* (29 November 1998): 4.

48. Marty Crisp, "Borders Books a Best Seller, Bailey White," Lancaster New Era (PA) (21 April 1996). *NewsBank NewsFile Collection* <http://www.infoweb.newsbank.com> (22 July 2000)

49. Shannon Maughan, "The Pinkwater Effect," *Publisher's Weekly* (25 January 1999): 30.

50. Shannon Maughan, "The 'Crocodile' files," *Publisher's Weekly* (29 November 1999): 41.

51. Pinkwater has recently expanded his activities as a reviewer of children's books by writing reviews and columns for Contentville <http://www.contentville.com> (1 September 2000).

52. Pinkwater's interest in automobiles goes 'way back, and vintage cars are featured in many of his books. His 1981 picture book, *Tooth-Gnasher Superflash*, tells of an automobile with some unexpected features. Professor McFwain's Hindustan-eight (*Yobgorgle*), Winston Bongo's 1958 Peugeot, (*Baconburg*) and Borgel's 1937 Dorbzeldge sedan are among the vehicles providing unexpected entertainment in Pinkwater's fiction.

53. Blackburn, 3.

Chapter 2

Three Decades of Fabulous Picture Books

Many relationships can be traced between Daniel Pinkwater's picture books and his longer stories, among them his young adult novels. However, becoming the famous author of a large and diverse body of work for readers of all ages was far off in the unimaginable future when Pinkwater began his writing career at the age of twenty-eight. During his first five years as an author, all of Pinkwater's publications were picture books with straightforward story lines, few characters, and simple illustrations. But within a few years, while he continued to produce picture books, Pinkwater also began writing stories with lengthier text passages and more complex situations.

The vast majority of Pinkwater's picture books are distinctive and unique. Some characters, places, and situations appear in multiple books, but the reader's overall impression is of a rich and impressive variety. There are a few consistent elements, and most of these elements characterize the author's stories and novels for older readers as well. Nearly all of the picture books are humorous, and the majority include fantasy elements such as talking animals, magical machines, or space travel. Certain admirable qualities such as individualism, creativity, and an adventurous disposition to try new experiences are consistently lauded.

Pinkwater's first book, *The Terrible Roar* (1970) is about a little lion who causes something to disappear each time he opens his mouth and roars. One reviewer described the illustrations as "exceedingly bright, flat-planed, simple and humorous color pictures which preschoolers will love."[1] Another critic considered *The Terrible Roar* to be the most cleverly illustrated of all of Pinkwater's picture books through 1989.

The roar itself is depicted as smaller and smaller circles or solid disks of color laid atop each other so that their bottom edges almost touch. The image effectively suggests the roar's echoes as well as the idea

13

of disappearance; the ever smaller circles seem to regress into infinity.[2]

Several of Pinkwater's picture books include episodes closely matching autobiographical sketches the author broadcast on National Public Radio. Many of these were collected in *Fish Whistle* (1989) and *Chicago Days, Hoboken Nights* (1991), both reprinted in *Hoboken Fish and Chicago Whistle* (1999). Pinkwater's second book, *Bear's Picture*, (1972) tells of an artist—who happens to be a brown bear—painting outdoors. Several critical onlookers, who have the appearance of identical tuxedo-clad penguins, make rude and ignorant comments about the painting and say that it doesn't look like what the bear claims to be drawing. "'It doesn't have to,'" said the bear, 'it is my picture.'" The penguins remain scornful, "But the bear looked at his picture and was happy."[3] In one of his commentaries, Pinkwater discusses his experiences as an art teacher. "This is an actual dialogue I overheard between two of the kids: 'That's not a motorcycle! It doesn't look anything like a motorcycle to me!' 'It doesn't have to. It's my picture.'" Pinkwater goes on to note approvingly that he learned a lot from such students.[4]

Pinkwater's picture book, *Doodle Flute* (1991), gives the impression of having been written by someone familiar with the instrument. In an essay, Pinkwater tells us that he played the flute for many years: "I stayed with the flute through military school, and junior high, and high school."[5] Another of his autobiographical essays recounts an unvarnished version of essentially the same story that Pinkwater had previously fictionalized as *Jolly Roger, a Dog of Hoboken* (1985).[6]

Doodle Flute and *Jolly Roger* are examples of a strand of autobiographical realism that is just as strong in Pinkwater's fiction as are the science fiction and fantasy elements for which he is better known. In fact, a number of Pinkwater's picture books are entirely realistic, while others, such as *Bear's Picture*, are straightforward except for the substitution of talking animals for humans. That device, of course, has a venerable literary heritage, through Aesop's *Fables*, Chaucer's *Nun's Priest's Tale*, the Grimm Brothers' *Fairy Tales*, and George Orwell's *Animal Farm*. Some of Pinkwater's stories raise the expectation of fantasy but turn out to have natural explanations. *The Phantom of the Lunch Wagon* (1992) is such a picture book, and the young adult novel, *The Snarkout Boys and the Avocado of Death* (also 1992) contains an equally surprising and pleasing explanation for a series of mysterious events.

Following *The Terrible Roar* and *Bear's Picture*, Pinkwater's third book was *Wizard Crystal* (1973). A wizard, who has "been unhappy every day for 307 years"[7] believes that whoever possesses a certain magic crystal will always be happy. Indeed, the ordinary frogs who inhabit a pond in which the crystal lies are exceptionally content. By his arts, the wizard locates the crystal at the bottom of the frogs' pond and takes it home. "How easy it is to get the thing which will make you happy!" he thinks. The frogs miss their crystal, and that night they travel to the wizard's house, surround it, and sing in their croaking way. The wizard dreams while the frogs sing, and when he awakens "he was not unhappy any more. He was not a wizard any more either. He was a frog." In the final illustration, we see that the wizard's home has disappeared, and that he is now living in a frog pond just like the pond from which he had taken the crystal.

This deceptively simple tale must have been influenced by Pinkwater's Zen studies. The Wizard is a Frog Prince in reverse: he achieves nirvana by merging with Nature rather than by separating from or overcoming her. This is in direct contrast with the typical Western quest-struggle, in which the hero must forge his personality by deeds which set him apart as a worthy individual. *Wizard Crystal* is a wise and haunting story, told with praiseworthy economy, and it is a strong accomplishment for a beginning author.

Some of Pinkwater's picture books of the 1970s resonate deeply with readers. *The Big Orange Splot* (1977) is often mentioned as a favorite. Passing over a block of identical homes, a seagull drops a can of orange paint on Mr. Plumbean's house. Instead of removing the paint, Mr. Plumbean is inspired to paint his house and decorate his yard in a vivid, exotic manner. The yard becomes a lush tropical paradise, featuring an adult alligator among rainforest vegetation. The neighbors urge one another to approach Mr. Plumbean, saying, "Tell him that his house has to be the same as ours so we can have a neat street."[8] One by one, each visits Mr. Plumbean in his wild and magical place, with the intent of reforming him, but each returns to decorate his own home in a different, but equally imaginative manner. They begin to echo Mr. Plumbean's refrain, "My house is me and I am it. My house is where I like to be and it looks like all my dreams."

With a few simple words and illustrations, *The Big Orange Splot* celebrates the joy of liberating the creative imagination. Even the dullest-seeming suburbanite has dreams that, if given expression, can enrich his own life and inspire his neighbors. A chance, shocking splash of bright orange paint may be needed to disrupt the stifling routines of social conformity that routinely suppress those latent imaginative instincts.[9]

By the mid-1970s, Pinkwater was writing not only longer picture books, but also stories for older readers. From *Wingman* in 1975, through *Young Adult Novel* in 1985, Pinkwater produced some sixteen titles for the middle-grade and young adult market, while maintaining his steady output of picture books. As he began writing novels and lengthier stories, some of the elaboration and complexity that is possible in those expanded formats began to appear in his picture books as well.

Fat Elliot and the Gorilla (1974) is the first of Pinkwater's longer and more elaborate picture books. The story is illustrated in much the same manner as *Wizard Crystal*, with rather simple black-and-white drawings, set in colored frames. However, *Fat Elliot* contains far more text than that earlier fable, as well as a larger cast of characters and a more complex plot. Young Elliot is unpopular and unhappy because he is very fat. His parents are indulgent and his doctor cynical about the situation. "You ought to go on a diet," the doctor said, but "of course nobody ever sticks to one." Then the doctor gives him a lollipop.[10] Elliot finds some non-human helpers: a wise-cracking weight scale and an imaginary gorilla, both of whom become his fitness coaches. In the end Elliot loses weight, feels better about himself, and begins to make friends. This is one of the few books in which Pinkwater approaches didacticism. The story's refrain, "You don't have to be what you don't want to be" is essentially its moral.

The persistently negative attitude toward obesity in *Fat Elliot* is also untypical. In his later books, Pinkwater is much more equivocal about the condition. While fat characters are sometimes lampooned in his stories—particularly if their obesity is clearly caused by self-indulgence—the satire usually has an affectionate tone. Pinkwater often conveys an appreciation for the Falstaffian grandeur of characters who live large. He once told an interviewer, "Fat people are, in fact, funny. In the same way that there's something delightful about elephants standing on their hind legs and doing tricks for the circus. There's a kind of joyousness to big, ponderous creatures."[11]

Following *Fat Elliot and the Gorilla*, Pinkwater brought out the first of his beloved Blue Moose stories. *The Blue Moose* (1975) and its sequels *Return of the Moose* (1979) and *The Moosepire* (1986) are all narrative-driven. This is by contrast with those basic thirty-two-page picture books having just a few simple words—*The Big Orange Splot*, for one—which are really carried by their illustrations. In such books, the words support the pictures, much like movie subtitles. However, Pinkwater's longer picture books, such as *Fat Elliott* and the Blue Moose trilogy, contain substantial text passages and can stand as effective stories without reference to the drawings.[12]

The Blue Moose is similar to *Bear's Picture* in that nothing occurring in the story is fantastic or unnatural except for the presence of a talking animal. However, this half-ton, bright blue, fully-antlered, moody and erudite bull moose makes quite an impact. Whereas the animals of *Bear's Picture* are simply substitutes for humans, the Blue Moose is a real moose, whose indoor presence and behavior startles the story's human characters.

The Moose is a marvelous creation, a rich personality full of virtues, vices, and eccentricities. A superb assistant in Mr. Breton's restaurant, yet rather full of himself and inclined to put on the airs of a haughty Parisian waiter in this humble north woods café, the Blue Moose is the first of Pinkwater's great fictional personalities. Michelle Landsberg noted, "Children's humor thrives on role reversal, and here a shy and insecure restaurateur, the good-hearted little Mr. Breton, blooms into prosperity after the moose moves in and takes on the job of headwaiter, bullying the customers with time-honored headwaiter hauteur."[13] The Blue Moose will be followed by Aunt Lulu, Uncle Melvin, Mush, Young Larry, and many other colorful characters, both human and animal, in Pinkwater's later picture books.

The Return of the Moose (1979) is the hilarious story of the Blue Moose's brief career as a novelist. He undergoes all the angst of a tormented artist, becoming even moodier than usual when he suffers a crisis of writer's block. Finally, he gets back on track, pounding away on a manual typewriter with his huge hooves, and all is sunshine. Mr. Breton is appalled by the Moose's ridiculous manuscript—it's full of outrageous braggadocio and accompanied by horribly crude drawings—but he doesn't want to hurt the Moose's feelings. With supreme confidence, the Moose sends the manuscript off to a publisher. To the surprise of everyone but the Moose, the manuscript is accepted for publication. The Moose takes on all the affectations of a successful author and soon becomes impossible in the restaurant: "Several times, when the customers handed their menus to the moose, after looking at them, the moose would sign his autograph on the menu, and hand them back to the customers."[14]

However, when the book is finally published, the story has been completely altered, and the jacket bears the sensational banner, "Hot Moose Love!" The Moose goes berserk, breaks into the printer's warehouse and eats every copy of the offending book before they can be distributed. The publisher is ultimately persuaded to publish the book exactly as originally submitted, and of course it becomes a bestseller. Soon afterward, the Moose is off to Hollywood.

This story is the best kind of sequel; rather than simply extending the original story, it uses the setting and characters of the original tale as a base from which to strike off in a fruitful new direction. The first Blue Moose story is a comedy, but the second is a satire. Everything in the story is a delightful send-up of the whole business of writing and publishing. This is a topic about which we can presume Pinkwater is fairly knowledgeable, having published some seventy books with perhaps twenty publishers and dozens of editors.

The third entry in the Blue Moose series, *The Moosepire* (1986) is even more self-referential than *The Return of the Moose*. In it, Pinkwater appears as himself, and we find him listening to the tale of Sir Charles Pacamac, "World's Champion Samovar Crasher," in the lounge of a private London club. Sir Charles tells Pinkwater an amazing story about a Blue Moose who claimed to have solved the mystery of Deadly Eric, a vampire moose who preyed upon citizens of Yellowtooth[15] in the rugged Canadian North. Pinkwater is so taken by this tale that he sets out for Yellowtooth immediately to investigate. Upon arrival, the author and explorer enters the local public library and proudly announces to the librarian,

> "I am Daniel Pinkwater, famous author and noted mooseologist."
> "I know all about that," Mildred Beeswax said. "You wrote those silly books about the Blue Moose."
> "Ah," I said, flattered, "then you have my books in this library?"
> "No."
> "Not even one?"
> "No. I won't have them in my library. We have standards here."[16]

After several further insults, Ms. Beeswax finally allows the author—if his hands are clean—to examine a manuscript left by the Blue Moose, "The Case of the Vampire Moose." It begins, "In order to escape unwanted publicity created by the books written by that fool, Pinkwater, I was forced to move to the northernmost wilderness. Fortunately, not many copies of the books were sold, and it looked as though I would be able to return to my normal life in a short time."[17] A long and ridiculous "shaggy dog" story ensues, in which it finally turns out that Deadly Eric was actually the Blue Moose himself, mistaken for a vampire moose by some of the more imaginative residents of Yellowtooth. (There's not much entertainment in those parts.)[18]

As he departs the Canadian wilderness, Pinkwater manages one final bit of self parody: "I was now ready to write another book about the

Blue Moose, and earn fame and vast sums of money by doing so."[19] Anyone who has read Pinkwater's essays and interview responses concerning the profession of writing children's books will be aware that this is a heavily ironic remark.

One other notable aspect of *The Moosepire* deserves mention. During a brief period in the middle 1980s, Pinkwater published several books with computer-generated illustrations, one of which was *The Moosepire*. The others are *Jolly Roger, a Dog of Hoboken* (1985), *The Muffin Fiend*, and *The Frankenbagel Monster* (both 1986, along with *The Moosepire*.) *Young Adults* (1985) contains similar illustrations. The dust wrapper of *Jolly Roger* explains that the computer drawings were created with an Apple Macintosh computer and the MacPaint program, and printed with a dot matrix printer.

During the mid-1980s personal computers were just coming into popular usage, and Pinkwater's extensive experimentation with the medium at this early stage of its development, after he had already proved himself a successful book illustrator over some fifteen years, is an intriguing departure. These 1985-1986 publications are Pinkwater's only books with computer art. During the following decade, Pinkwater went back to his usual technique of hand-illustrating his books with bright felt markers, often supplemented by lines rendered with a black ink pen. Jill Pinkwater took over the artwork in 1996, and although her style is distinct, she also favors felt markers.

Ducks! is a curious picture book of the mid-1980s that Pinkwater illustrated with colored markers rather than with his Macintosh. Young Scott is persuaded to free a talking duck who turns out to be an angel. Scott escorts the duck to heaven and is offered the opportunity to become an angel himself, but decides that he would rather go back to earth and be alive. The matter-of-fact handling of death in this children's story is unusual and quite commendable. Scott's parents are quite droll, especially his mother, who sports spiky green-tipped hair and an "I ♥ Rock N' Roll" t-shirt.[20]

During the late 1970s and early 1980s three of Pinkwater's books were illustrated by other artists: *Around Fred's Bed* (1976) by Robert Mertens, *The Wuggie Norple Story* (1980) by the great Tomie de Paola, and *Roger's Umbrella* (1982) by James Marshall. All of Pinkwater's other books through 1996—about thirty picture books and several illustrated stories for intermediate readers—were illustrated by the author himself. Besides the felt marker and computer illustrations previously mentioned, Pinkwater's other artwork includes several varieties of monochrome illustrations, including line drawings with black ink (*Wizard Crystal*, 1973), and greytone illustrations in which intermediate shades supplement the black line drawings (*Magic Camera*, 1974; *Return of the Moose*, 1979). *Lizard Music*, uniquely, is illustrated with the author's block prints. Pinkwater has produced only a few hand-illustrated monochrome picture books; the majority are quite colorful.

A pair of Pinkwater's vivid picture books from the late 1980s present some unusual relatives: *Aunt Lulu* (1988) and *Uncle Melvin* (1989). Like Mildred Beeswax, Aunt Lulu is a librarian in the far North. But she's far more likeable than the tart Ms. Beeswax. Each week Lulu hitches up her sled and her fourteen huskies, and delivers books to gold miners out at their diggings in Alaska.[21] Aunt Lulu, one of Pinkwater's best female characters, is a tough and resourceful woman, undeterred by cold, snow, and blizzards. Nevertheless, she eventually tires of Alaska, and decides to relocate to Parsippany, New Jersey, where the narrator, her nephew, lives with his family. Naturally, her fourteen huskies insist upon moving with her. She arrives during winter and continues using her sled team in Parsippany. The family wonders what she will do when it gets warm. When she finally gets to take off her parka and mukluks, we find that Lulu can be quite a fashionable woman. She and her fourteen huskies happily pose in front of a Parsippany ice cream stand, all fifteen of them wearing matching sunglasses with pink frames.[22]

Both Aunt Lulu and her huskies are drawn with real affection. We can't help but like them.[23] It's a pleasure to see that Aunt Lulu is a perfectly attractive and feminine woman, despite her toughness in Alaska, and her status as an unmarried librarian—often an unfortunate stereotype. Significantly, Pinkwater dedicates *Aunt Lulu* "To *good* librarians everywhere," (italics Pinkwater's) which may suggest that he has met both good and bad ones.

Uncle Melvin is quite a different character. A gentle soul, his mental condition requires that he reside in some sort of halfway house which he calls the "Looney Bin."[24] The narrator is Melvin's nephew, a boy named Charles. Uncle Melvin is completely trusted by Charles' parents, and spends most of his days at their house, where he does housework, walks Charles to school, and works in the garden. Melvin is eccentric and harbors a number of apparent delusions, including conspiracy theories and the beliefs that he can hold two-way conversations with birds and animals and influence the weather.

Although the title character of *Uncle Melvin* is prone to fantasies, there is a tremendous realism to the triangular relationship between Charles, Uncle Melvin, and Charles's parents. An important dialogue revolves around the triangle. Uncle Melvin tells Charles that he can talk with birds, make it rain, and cause rainbows. Charles, as a child naturally would, runs to his father and asks whether these things are possible. The father gives a wonderful reply, conveying great affection and respect for his brother, and while acknowledging Melvin's affinity with wildlife, he unequivocally states that Melvin cannot influence the weather. Again very plausibly, young Charles goes right back to Melvin, and says, "My father doesn't believe you can do that stuff with the rain." Melvin's reply is entirely characteristic: "That's okay," Melvin said. "I wouldn't believe it myself." Some days later, Charles looks outside after a rainfall. Uncle Melvin is working in the garden. Birds are hopping around him as usual, and there are four rainbows in the sky.

The ambiguity as to whether Uncle Melvin is completely delusional is characteristic of Pinkwater's handling of supernatural topics. In the 1983 picture book, *I Was a Second Grade Werewolf*, young Lawrence Talbot wakes up one morning and finds he has changed into a werewolf. He sees himself in the mirror as a werewolf and behaves the part. In the book's illustrations, we, too, see him as a werewolf and we also see a picture of iron bars he has bent with his superhuman strength. Yet none of the other characters in the story—his mother, teachers, or friends—seem aware of his transformation. After returning to his normal appearance Lawrence tells us, "Nobody had noticed anything. The next time I turn into a werewolf, it's going to be different."[25] The story is cute and funny. However, it also conveys a sense of how strange and lonely it is to experience some powerful change which makes you feel entirely different, but to have nobody show any awareness that today you are not the same person you were yesterday.

Devil in the Drain (1984) presents another sort of ambiguous supernatural character. An unnamed boy discovers a little orange-red devil in his kitchen drain. While conversing with the devil, it turns out that the boy had once accidentally lost a goldfish down that same drain. We are shown a picture of the unfortunate goldfish, which looks suspiciously similar to the little devil. Along with his other annoying behaviors, the devil tries to make the boy feel guilty over the goldfish accident. The boy rejects the devil's attempts to "guilt-trip" him, and he finally flushes the obnoxious demon back down the drain. As in *I Was a Second Grade Werewolf*, the supernatural character in *Devil in the Drain* can be read as an aspect of the protagonist's own psyche; his superego, in Freudian terms. More simply put, the devil represents the boy's capacity for tormenting himself with needless guilt. Fortunately, the boy has a healthy self-image and flushes the temptation away.[26]

Another boy with an active imagination for monsters is featured in a picture book of the early 1990s, *Wempires* (1991). Pinkwater has populated his stories with just about every variety of scary monster, including ghosts, devils, werewolves, and vampires. Young Jonathan is obsessed with vampires, and loves putting on vampire regalia, including plastic vampire teeth. One day he brings home the following note from school: "Dear Mrs. Harker, Jonathan has been threatening to bite children in his class. I have asked him to leave his fangs at home. I hope you will have a little talk with him. Yours truly, Mildred Van Helsing (Teacher)."[27] Jonathan Harker and Professor Van Helsing are, of course, characters in Bram Stoker's novel, *Dracula*.

In *Wempires*, it is clear to all that young Jonathan is not a real vampire, but just a child undergoing a temporary enthusiasm. However, after delivering the teacher's note, Jonathan is visited in the middle of the night by three middle-aged men in capes and brightly-colored tennis shoes, who call themselves "Wempires." The odd variation on the word "vampire" is explained by their Yiddish accents. They disclaim any interest in blood, ("Drinking blood—yich!") and prove that they prefer normal food by going down to the kitchen with Jonathan and raiding his family's refrigerator for a midnight snack of chicken and ginger ale. As they descend the staircase, we see that they are wearing colorful sneakers under their capes.

Jonathan's mother is wakened by their party. "What's this? Vampires in the kitchen in the middle of the night?" She briskly shoos the Wempires out of the house, complains about the mess they have made ("There are crumbs everywhere"), and says to Jonathan, "Now do you see why your father and I didn't want you to behave like a vampire?" Apparently, because it could lead to no less an evil than the littering of their kitchen with the remains of late-night snacks! In contrast to the obnoxious title character of *Devil in the Drain*, the Wempires are fun-loving party guys. Jonathan concludes, "What neat guys! Nothing will ever change my mind about being a vampire."

The story validates Jonathan's fascination with mythological monsters. It celebrates the role of romantic, adventurous stories and the identification with fantasy heroes in the formation of a child's personality. Of course Jonathan doesn't want anyone to be hurt, he's just fascinated by the scariness and glamour of vampire mythology. The story begins, "I saw a movie on TV one Saturday afternoon. It was about a vampire. What a good movie! The vampire was scary. He was real smooth. I liked his clothes. I decided I would be a vampire." Like youngsters everywhere, Jonathan wants to play at trying on adventurous costumes and personas. The book is dedicated "To F.W. Murnau," (1888-1931), the German Expressionist director of *Nosferatu* (1922), a great silent film version of Bram Stoker's *Dracula*.

Several more of Pinkwater's books have titles pertaining to monsters, including a pair of the computer-illustrated books previously mentioned. *The Muffin Fiend* (1986) may have been influenced by the 1984 film *Amadeus*. In the picture book, Wolfgang Amadeus Mozart is a detective as well as a composer, and he assists Inspector Charles Le-Chat (Charles the Cat, named for Pinkwater's own "office cat")[28] Despite being called a "fiend," the muffin thief is not really a monster, but an extraterrestrial. How did Mozart make this deduction? "I knew because no one on Earth would eat a Gorgonzola muffin."[29]

The book is full of amusing puns and gags. At one point the detectives are searching the Vienna Woods: "There was nothing out of the ordinary to be seen in the woods. The usual birds and animals were in evidence, and the trees of course, and the odd peasant."[30] meaning, of course, an occasional peasant. But in the next scene, the detectives interview a single "odd peasant." When the muffin thief is finally found, the musical dialogue which ensues between Mozart and "Don Pastrami" follows the libretto of Mozart's opera, *Don Giovanni*.

The Frankenbagel Monster (also 1986) is inspired by Mary Shelley's famous novel, *Frankenstein* (1818) and the many derivative films featuring a half-human monster created by the deranged Baron Frankenstein. Here the obsessed bagel maker Harold Frankenbagel creates a huge mechanical bagel monster, the Glimville Bagelunculus. As in *The Muffin Fiend*, the quest for a monster turns out to be an elaborate shaggy dog story to set up a silly gag. Wise old Professor Von Sweeney has stopped the monster bagel in the middle of its rampage by loudly threatening to eat it. The chastened and relieved Frankenbagel asks,

"But how did you know that it would go stale like that?"
"Just a matter of experience," says Professor Von Sweeney. "Bagels always go stale just before you're ready to eat them—everyone knows that. I simply assumed that this universal truth would apply to your monster bagel."[31]

Another of Pinkwater's picture books with a spooky title, *The Phantom of the Lunch Wagon* (1992), threatens to present a scary specter. Strange noises are heard at a restored diner, and customers are frightened away. Old Mr. Wiggers remembers that the original lunch wagon had closed because of a phantom. He tells the new owner that, "Compared to a phantom, a ghost is a joke."[32] However, when Mr. Wiggers and owner Chris Kevin-Keith finally summon the courage to seek out the phantom, they discover nothing but a small white cat living in the lunch wagon's basement.

In addition to monsters, of course Pinkwater is also noted for his use of science fiction themes. Half a dozen of his books include the word "space" in their titles. The earliest is *Fat Men From Space* (1977), a middle-grade book which Pinkwater once described as his most commercially successful publication.[33] The other five are picture books from the late nineteen-eighties through the mid-nineties. *Guys From Space* (1989) is dedicated "To Charles, a cat, even though he threw up on my computer printer."[34] *Guys From Space* has some elements in common with *Borgel*, a novel Pinkwater published a year later. In both stories, a boy suddenly has an opportunity to travel in outer space, and in both, he comes across a root beer stand run by a large ugly alien creature. The two stories must have been on Pinkwater's desk at about the same time.

Spaceburger (1993), another picture book with "space," in its title, turns out not to involve extraplanetary travel or any other paranormal phenomena. In this story, Pinkwater presents the opening of an imaginary new fast food franchise based upon an outer space theme.[35] The food at the Spaceburger outlet is the usual sort of burger and fries fast food, but the architecture and ambience of the place are distinctive. Since the outer space craze in America occurred during the 1950s and 1960s, the story is more a nostalgic throwback to the early McDonald's era of the author's youth than a depiction of current popular culture tastes.

Ned Feldman, Space Pirate (1994) is one of Pinkwater's longer picture books, with substantial text passages in its forty-eight pages. The story has elements in common with several of the author's other books, but it combines them in a unique manner. The story begins with young Ned discovering a little alien and his spaceship in the cupboard under the kitchen sink, a setting reminiscent of *Devil in the Drain*. An ensuing trip into outer space is of course a familiar Pinkwater event. The supposedly intrepid "Captain Bugbeard" turns out to be childishly enthusiastic about costumes, and a coward, rather like *Yobgorgle*'s Uncle Mel. On an unknown planet, Ned and the Captain discover enormous but stupid and harmless giant chickens, much like Henrietta of *The Hoboken Chicken Emergency*. When Ned returns from his adventure, we find that his parents have been at a professional wrestling match (echoes of the Snarkout novels.) When Ned tells his parents that he's been on a trip to outer space, his parents smile indulgently and humor what they suppose to be his fantasies, exactly as the boy's mother does in *Guys From Space*.

Jill Pinkwater, herself the author of several excellent children's books as well as a talented visual artist, has illustrated all of her husband's picture books in recent years, beginning with *Wallpaper From Space* in 1996. Her drawings greatly enhance this story of a boy who has a wonderful outer space experience after his bedroom has been decorated by his thoughtful mother with glow-in-the dark nighttime stars and planets. The book is attractively designed and illustrated, with lovely and colorful flourishes to the chapter headings and page numbers, and charming drawings in many different sizes and shapes arranged around the text.[36] Steve's dream-fantasy has something of the surrealistic magic of Maurice Sendak's *In the Night Kitchen*. The witty decorative elements provided by Jill Pinkwater are perfectly suited to the story's wallpaper motif.

Another recent Pinkwater story with a space theme and title is *Mush, a Dog From Space* (1995). This delightful picture book has a number of pleasing features. Both the narrator, a girl named Kelly Mangiaro, and the "dog from space," Mush, are female. This is a welcome departure for Pinkwater. It happens to be the last book he illustrated himself before Jill Pinkwater took over the drawings for Daniel's books, so he must be accorded full credit for the inclusion of strong female characters in this story.[37]

Mush, evidently a malamute, but calling herself a "mushamute," is full of personality. Her interactions with humans are much in the vein of the Blue Moose; like him she is a bit of a prima donna, with an amused tolerance for the humans who are so astonished by her abilities. The story also features some excellent satire on the modern American family. Both of Kelly's parents work, but the extra income has not added graciousness to the family's lifestyle. One problem is that the parents are too busy to get to the grocery store. However, since Kelly's mother works at a factory that packages frozen chicken dinners, the freezer is always full of her company's products, if little else. Much of the story's humor revolves around the contrast of Mush's gourmet presentations with the usual haphazard fare at the Mangiaro home.

In concluding our survey of Pinkwater's "space fiction," it should be noted that the publishers of *Mush, a Dog From Space* seem to have considered that subset of the author's works to be a meaningful category. One of the prefatory pages of *Mush* contains the following legend:

Pinkwater's guides to the galaxy
Borgel
Guys from Space
Spaceburger
Ned Feldman, Space Pirate[38]

This "pseudo-series" title is, of course, suggestive of the title of Douglas Adams' popular best-seller, *The Hitchhiker's Guide to the Galaxy* (1979). Not a bad idea to drop such a hint, since most Adams enthusiasts would probably enjoy the works of Pinkwater, and vice-versa. In view of Pinkwater's enduring interest in space fiction, it is not surprising that his first young adult novel, *Alan Mendelsohn, the Boy from Mars* (1979) includes an extraterrestrial adventure.

One other picture book of the early 1990s must be mentioned. *Author's Day* (1993) is a book of exceptional charm. As self-referential in its own way as *The Return of the Moose* and *The Moosepire*, *Author's Day* is the story of a scheduled visit to a grade school by an author of books for children. The book is full of amusing details such as the pile of styrofoam coffee cups littering the floor of the author's battered car. Everyone there has confused him with another children's author, and they keep referring to that other author's books and characters so persistently that our author is finally compelled to give up and go along with the error. He is escorted upon a whirlwind tour of several classrooms, in each of which the children behave appropriately to their age.

The visit is something of an ordeal, despite everyone's good nature. The sixth-graders, who have the appearance of juvenile delinquents in training, nearly succeed in tying the author with ropes. In a perfect ending, a second-grader asks the author as he is leaving, "Do you think you might ever write a book about us?"[39] A recent article by children's author Roland Smith used the book as the basis for a light-hearted but genuine discussion of the do's and don'ts of author visits, noting that despite its humorous tone, Pinkwater's story does a rather good job of covering some of the genuine hazards of the situation.

> When I pack for a school visit I take signing pens; slides; bookmarks; brochures . . . a rubber hot dog; anti-bacterial hand goo; and a copy of *Author's Day* by Daniel Pinkwater, which cheers me up every time I read it.
>
> Years ago, at one of my author's visits, my hosts gave me a copy of Mr. Pinkwater's book. I started reading it back at the hotel and laughed so hard I got a call from the front desk asking if I was okay. . . . I called my wife, Marie, and read the entire book to her over the phone.[40]

Most of Pinkwater's picture books of the late 1990s belong to one or another of two series. *Young Larry* (1997) is the first of four books to date about a polar bear of that name. The story begins with Larry and his brother as cubs, and includes some clever and accurate natural history.[41] Early in the story, the cubs' affectionate mother tells them that one day she'll hit them in the head and from that time they'll have to fend for themselves. "Wow. That is harsh," they reply. She tells them, "That's Nature's way. Get used to it." A year or so later, "The day finally came when Larry and Roy's mother called them to her, and hit each of them in the head. 'Get lost,' she said. 'Go and fend for yourselves.' Then she went away to see what Larry and Roy's father was doing."[42] A more compact and matter-of-fact presentation of reproductive behavior within a book for children can hardly be imagined.

Larry and Roy are happily reunited in *At the Hotel Larry* (1997). Jill Pinkwater's flat, colorful illustrations of the bears are reminiscent of the posters of Toulouse-Lautrec and the paintings of Henri Matisse and other Fauve artists of the early twentieth century.[43] This kind of sight gag—occasionally used by both Pinkwaters in their art—is the visual equivalent of Pinkwater's insertion of historical names into his text. If the reader catches the reference, so much the better, but there's no interruption of the narrative or loss of meaning for those who miss the joke.[44]

Bongo Larry (1998) provided Pinkwater an opportunity to introduce young readers to the beatnik scene, which flavored two of the author's young adult novels, *The Snarkout Boys and the Baconburg Horror* and *The Education of Robert Nifkin*. At the beginning of the story, Larry is undergoing a rebellious phase, and he behaves rudely to a policeman, to the dismay of Mr. Frobisher.[45] Eventually, Larry "mellows out," as he gets the opportunity to perform on his bongos at the Café Mama Bear. As one reviewer noted, "Larry has the attributes of a real bear as well as a talking cartoon. . . . Yet the Pinkwaters resist lapsing into teddy-bear cuteness; Larry is edgy and likable without being too cuddly."[46] Precisely; that "edginess" is what makes Larry, along with Mush and the Blue Moose, such compelling animal characters. All of the Young Larry stories are quite satisfying.

In the most recent, *Ice Cream Larry*, the inventive bear creates a codfish-flavored ice cream bar, surely a culinary achievement to rival Steve Nickelson's olive milkshakes (*Attila the Pun*), and the Gorgonzola muffins of *The Muffin Fiend*.[47]

The Potato Kids series also included four imprints during the late 1990s. These stories involve the interracial friendship of second-graders Big Bob and Big Gloria. All four of the stories are centered upon holiday celebrations, into which Big Gloria always intrudes her favorite food item, the potato. The little books in this formula series are competently executed and are not without some charm. However, they

lack the imaginative flair of Pinkwater's non-serial fiction, and they are
certainly not representative of his true genius as a children's author.[48]
    In addition to the Young Larry and Potato Kids series, the Pink-
waters brought out other picture books during the late 1990s. *Wolf
Christmas* (1998) has an obvious holiday connection, like all of the
Potato Kids stories, but it is a much more original work. The narrator is
a young female wolf, and all of the wolves' actions are quite natural to
their species. On "the longest night of the year," a family of eight
wolves races through the snowy woods and finally looks down upon a
human village, from which they can faintly hear the singing of Christmas carols. The wolves lift their muzzles to the sky and sing as well.[49]
The book is a "mood piece" or "tone poem;" it captures a special moment of time when all is peaceful and harmonious, and renders it with
great beauty. We are told that the wolves had already eaten a dinner of
venison prior to the story's opening, and so the interlude captured by
this narrative is a special moment free of strife. The book has earned
fine reviews:

> An offbeat solstice tale from the master of the offbeat is
> marvelously matched by his wife's distinctive felt-pen il-
> lustrations. . . . The author works wolf habits and lore into
> the simple dialogue . . . and the illustrator gives each wolf a
> distinctive look and personality. . . . The wolves, the snow,
> and the night sky make wonderful patterns on the pages,
> and the playful, anthropomorphic text will cheer and
> amuse.[50]

    Jill Pinkwater's drawings tend to be prettier and more polished
than her husband's. Both Pinkwaters have a talent for comic illustration, but Jill's artistry is preferable for a book such as *Wolf Christmas*,
where the mood is more romantic than humorous. Daniel Pinkwater has
a cartoonist's feel for caricature, and with a few quick lines he can con-
vey the essential aspect of a character. His drawings, although often
rather crude, appeal through their freshness and spontaneity. Part of
their charm is that they resemble a child's drawings, and seem appropriate for stories told from a child's point of view. They appear not to
have been labored over, and have been described as "deceptively simple."[51] Although Jill Pinkwater's illustrations are more "artistic" and
finished-looking than Daniel's, both artists are effective illustrators of
Daniel's texts, each in their respective styles.
    Another recent non-serial story, *Rainy Morning* (1998) is based
upon a "House That Jack Built" premise; that is, more and more characters are added to the story in a sort of ritualistic, hypnotic, sing-song

parade. On a very rainy day, Mr. and Mrs. Submarine first allow their cat and then their dog to come in and get dry. But more and more characters, some quite unlikely, keep wanting to come in, and each of them must be fed fresh corn muffins. One reviewer noted, "Daniel Pinkwater achieves sublime ridiculousness by showing the Submarine's limitless hospitality."[52]

The incremental piling on of characters in *Rainy Morning* is reminiscent of Pinkwater's *The Wuggie Norple Story* (1980) in which a kitten grows at such a tremendous rate that the family is unable to agree upon his size. In an attempt to judge the kitten's size by comparison, the father is moved to bring home successively larger animals each day to measure against the kitten. This sort of story provides a rationale for bringing in many different animal species to illustrate, much like the biblical story of Noah's Ark, long a favorite subject of artists who wish to showcase an ability to draw many species well.

The similarity of *Rainy Morning* to stories Pinkwater published two decades earlier bespeaks a fundamental continuity in the author's works. Pinkwater's picture books are rich and varied, but a single imagination lies behind the entire corpus. Most of the themes that will be developed in his novels are here: food and fatness, nonconformity, the power of the imagination, exotic travel, and appreciation for the magic to be found in our everyday lives. Like his longer stories and novels, Pinkwater's picture books are populated by unexpected combinations of fascinating characters: human, animal, fantastic, and extraterrestrial.

NOTES

1. Ann D. Schweibish, "The Terrible Roar," *School Library Journal* (March 1971): 23.
2. Janice M. Alberghene, in *Twentieth-Century Children's Writers*, 3rd ed. (Chicago: St. James Press, 1989), 782.
3. Daniel Pinkwater, *Bear's Picture*. (New York: E.P. Dutton, 1972).
4. Daniel Pinkwater, *Hoboken Fish and Chicago Whistle* (Princeton, N.J.: Xlibris, 1999), 184.
5. *Hoboken Fish*, 306.
6. *Hoboken Fish*, 325.
7. Daniel Pinkwater, *Wizard Crystal* (New York: Dodd & Mead, 1973).
8. Daniel Pinkwater, *The Big Orange Splot* (New York: Hastings House, 1977).
9. Pinkwater recently offered a livelier explanation as to what is really going on in that story: "The secret message in *The Big Orange Splot* is that if you do enough eccentric things, you can keep a fairly large alligator as a pet, and your

neighbors won't insist you get rid of it!" *Talk to DP Forum The (Sort of) Official Daniel Pinkwater Website, Talk to DP Forum* <http://www designfoundry.com/p-zone> (5 June 2000).
10. Daniel Pinkwater, *Fat Elliot and the Gorilla* (New York: Four Winds Press, 1974).
11. Wann, *Fat!So?*
12. Paradoxically, the more advanced stories, those less dependent upon illustrations, are sometimes better suited for being read aloud to young children, especially when it is not convenient to display the pictures to the audience while reading.
13. Michelle Landsberg, *Reading for the Love of It* (New York: Prentice-Hall, 1986), 81.
14. Daniel Pinkwater, *The Blue Moose* (New York: Dodd & Mead, 1975), 43.
15. I.e., Yellowknife, the capital of Canada's Northwest Territories.
16. Daniel Pinkwater, *The Moosepire* (Boston: Little, Brown, 1986), 14.
17. *The Moosepire*, 18.
18. In one of the drawings, a wool-hatted and lumberjack-shirted townsman's contorted face and pained gesture parodies the well-known painting "The Scream" by the Norwegian painter Edvard Munch (1863-1944). The moose stands curiously in the moonlit background with a question mark over his antlers. *The Moosepire*, 32. See note 42, below, for Pinkwater's comments on such homages to famous paintings in his books.
19. *The Moosepire*, 44.
20. Daniel Pinkwater, *Ducks!* (Boston: Little, Brown, 1984).
21. Daniel Pinkwater, *Aunt Lulu* (New York: Macmillan, 1988).
22. Pinkwater's latest picture book, *The Magic Pretzel*, also features a dog wearing pink-framed glasses. Nine-year-old Lucy Fang is featured on Jill Pinkwater's cover illustration, in her werewolf form. Fortunately, Lucy's pink-framed glasses remain in place when she transforms, otherwise her parents would presumably need to buy new eyeglasses for her after every full moon. Lucy's ambition is "To be selected Miss America, and then bite the judges." Daniel Pinkwater, *The Magic Pretzel* (New York: Aladdin Paperbacks, 2000), 54.
23. Pinkwater has owned a number of dogs, including several malamutes. He tells a series of wonderful dog stories in *Fish Whistle*. (*Hoboken Fish*, 115-42). Northern dogs appear in several of his other stories, notably *The Magic Moscow* (1980) and *Mush: a Dog From Space* (1995). Both Daniel and Jill Pinkwater draw dogs and wolves with real understanding; their appreciation of the canine family comes through strongly in their respective illustrations.
24. Daniel Pinkwater, *Uncle Melvin* (New York: Macmillan, 1989).
25. Daniel Pinkwater, *I Was a Second Grade Werewolf* (New York: E. P. Dutton, 1983).
26. Daniel Pinkwater, *Devil In the Drain* (New York: E. P. Dutton, 1984).
27. Daniel Pinkwater, *Wempires* (New York: Macmillan, 1991).
28. "When Charles moved into the house, he appointed himself my office cat, helper and adviser." *Hoboken Fish*, 148.

29. Daniel Pinkwater, *The Muffin Fiend* (New York: Lothrop, Lee & Shepard, 1986), 47.

30. *The Muffin Fiend*, 29.

31. Daniel Pinkwater, *The Frankenbagel Monster* (New York: E. P. Dutton, 1986).

32. Daniel Pinkwater, *The Phantom of the Lunch Wagon* (New York: Macmillan, 1992).

33. In response to an email question, Pinkwater replied, "The title of mine that was the biggest seller (not that any of the books have been big in the RL Stine sense), is probably *Fat Men From Space*." *Talk to DP Forum, Archive,* 8 (29 October 1999).

34. Daniel Pinkwater, *Guys From Space* (New York: Macmillan, 1989).

35. Daniel Pinkwater, *Spaceburger* (New York: Macmillan, 1993).

36. Daniel Pinkwater, *Wallpaper From Space* (New York: Atheneum, 1996).

37. Daniel Pinkwater, *Mush, a Dog From Space* (New York: Atheneum, 1995).

38. *Mush, a Dog From Space*, unnumbered prefatory page.

39. Daniel Pinkwater, *Author's Day* (New York: Macmillan, 1993).

40. Roland Smith, "Author's Day Revisited." *Journal of Youth Services for Libraries* (fall 1999): 14-16.

41. Also some human history. A character in the story is named Mr. Martin Frobisher, in honor of the great English explorer of the Canadian Arctic, Sir Martin Frobisher (1535?-1594).

42. Daniel Pinkwater, *Young Larry* (New York: Marshall Cavendish, 1997).

43. Henri Matisse, Paul Gauguin, Pablo Picasso, Henry Rousseau, and other artists working during this period turned away from the blurred, mottled textures of Impressionist canvasses toward a bolder style influenced by Polynesian, Oriental, and African art. Depth and perspective were de-emphasized in these compositions built from strong, flat, sharply-delineated color segments. Matisse's bright paper cutouts are a culmination of this trend.

44. When asked about references to famous paintings in his own and his wife's illustrations, Pinkwater replied, "Probably there is more visual by-play than textual. I have a B. A. in Art, (not a BFA), and my wife is the daughter of a painter, and was dragged to museums from the age of naught. The Larry books are replete with many themes from Matisse, including the famous circle dance, "Danse," at the end of *At the Hotel Larry*. . . . You caught the Munch in *Moosepire*, but I bet you missed the stag from Albrecht Dürer. There are tons of references—we salt the books with them." Email from D. Pinkwater to W. Hogan, 4 May 2000.

45. Daniel Pinkwater, *Bongo Larry* (New York: Marshall Cavendish, 1998).

46. *Publisher's Weekly* (7 July 1997): 244.

47. Daniel Pinkwater, *Ice Cream Larry* (New York: Marshall Cavendish, 1999).

48. Pinkwater's first book of the 21st century, *The Magic Pretzel*, has opened yet another new series: it is #1 of "The Werewolf Club" series, with *The Lunchroom of Doom* announced as #2.

49. Daniel Pinkwater, *Wolf Christmas* (New York: Marshall Cavendish, 1998).

50. *Booklist* (1 September 1998): 134.
51. *Something About the Author* (Detroit: Gale Research, 1987), vol. 114, 158.
52. *Publisher's Weekly* (22 February 1999): 94.

Chapter 3

Seven Stories

During an astonishingly fertile eight-year period, while he was also publishing picture books and young adult novels, Daniel Pinkwater brought out ten of the eleven books he has written for the intermediate age group during his three-decade writing career. These include *Wingman* (1975), *Lizard Music* (1976), *The Hoboken Chicken Emergency* (1977), *Fat Men From Space* (1977), *The Last Guru* (1978), *Yobgorgle, Mystery Monster of Lake Ontario* (1979), *The Magic Moscow* (1980), *Attila the Pun* (1981), *The Worms of Kukumlima* (1981), and *Slaves of Spiegel* (1982).[1]

The longest of these—*Lizard Music, Yobgorgle,* and *The Worms of Kukumlima,* along with the later *Borgel* (1990)—are true novels, and will be examined in more detail in the next chapter. Many of the others could be called "illustrated stories." Although all were originally published as individual hardbound monographs, most of them are too short to be regarded as novels.

Before discussing these seven shorter works, we should also pause to consider the categories of "picture," "middle-grade," and "young adult" books. Why should we bother with these concepts? When asked about the marketing of his books to various age groups, Daniel Pinkwater responded, "I, personally, do not make any distinction, except that when writing for adults one ought to take into account their diminished intelligence and powers of concentration."[2] Later, he added,

> I have in mind neither children, young adults, adults or aged adults when I write. My intended readership is extraterrestrial space aliens. I don't know for sure whether any such beings are reading my work yet, but I think Amazon.com knows. If only I could get them to break their code of silence![3]

Despite Pinkwater's humorous disdain for such categories, two reasons for using them will be mentioned here. First, they are regularly employed by publishers, educators, librarians, reviewers, parents, and readers as a means of determining the age or grade range to which a book is targeted, and/or by whom it is most likely to be appreciated. The three broad classes of books for young persons are: (1) picture books/books for beginning readers; (2) books for middle-grade or intermediate-level readers (usually pre-adolescents); and (3) books for young adults (adolescents). These categories are often printed on the covers of books, are mentioned in book reviews, and are used by libraries and bookstores as a way of organizing literature for youth.

The second reason for using such categories in the present work is an immediately practical one. Since this is one of a series on "young adult literature," it was necessary to decide which of Daniel Pinkwater's many books should be the focus of our study. The half-dozen books judged to fit the category are each assigned a full chapter here (chapters 5-10). All have distinctly adolescent protagonists and themes, and some (*Young Adult Novel* and *Young Adults*) even have dead-giveaway titles!

Among Pinkwater's many other works, the books discussed in the previous chapter—most of them containing numerous illustrations and just a few simple words—are easy to identify as picture books. These are obviously far removed from the young adult category. But what about the author's eleven works of juvenile fiction that fall somewhere between?

Pinkwater's intermediate works of fiction share a number of characteristic features. As might be expected, these works stand midway between the author's picture books and his young adult novels with respect to length, reading difficulty, topical content, and illustrations. The seven shorter books average about eighty pages in length, while the four "expedition novels" are about twice that long.[4] By definition, all of these works contain much lengthier passages of text than are encountered in picture books for beginning readers. Even so, the grammar, vocabulary, and narrative flow of Pinkwater's middle-grade books are quite accessible to grade school readers, and all of them are well-suited for reading aloud to very young children.

Among Pinkwater's books, the amount of illustrative content reliably indicates the reading level: the more pictures, the lower the age range of the target audience. All of the picture books are, of course, profusely illustrated, the majority in strong, bright colors. Most of the shorter middle-grade works are also illustrated, but not so lavishly.[5] Each contains ten to twenty black-and-white drawings by the author.[6] The lone exception is *Slaves of Spiegel*, which has no artwork.[7] By contrast, the long middle-grade novels tend not to be illustrated. One of the four, *Lizard Music*, includes half a dozen of the author's black-and-white wood or linoleum block prints.[8] However, the other expedition novels, *Yobgorgle, The Worms of Kukumlima,* and *Borgel* are not illustrated, nor are any of Pinkwater's young adult novels.[9]

Beyond the general characteristics of book length, reading level, and illustrative content, one of the most notable qualities of Pinkwater's middle-grade fiction is the open, unsophisticated persona of the young protagonist in each of the stories.[10] He is always a pre-adolescent boy, nine to twelve years of age. In contrast to the angst-ridden adolescents who narrate the young adult novels, the heroes of the middle-grade books are usually rather ordinary, cheerful young fellows. This is partly due to their pre-teen innocence, and partly due to the fact that many of these stories take place during summer holidays, thus school—that oppressive bastion of conformity and mediocrity in Pinkwater's young adult novels—is usually not in the foreground. But there is more to it than that. Much of the comic effect of the middle-grade novels is provided by the narrators' simple, understated descriptions of eccentric adults and wild goings-on.

Typically, Pinkwater's young protagonist serves as a foil, or "straight man" for the antics of a number of ridiculous adult characters, who are variously gluttonous, badly dressed, wildly eccentric, or grossly incompetent. The narrator's low-key, dead-pan style enhances the comedy, as in Eugene Winkleman's musings about the two adults with whom he has been keeping company: "It occurred to me that I had been seen in the street with a guy wearing a cowboy suit and a guy dressed up as a chicken. A fat man in a Jungle-Jim suit was no worse. We went out."[11] Norman Bleistift's calm observations after being hijacked by aliens to another planet are equally understated: "They're having a sort of world's fair on Spiegel. It's pretty nice, and I saw a lot of very unusual things. Steve said it's really lucky for a kid of my age to get to visit another planet at all, let alone one on which there is a big fair and a cooking contest."[12] Later, Norman tells us: "What Tesev Noskecnil was supposed to cook was hot celery tonic soup, lead-dipped bagels, and mammoth goose legs. It's the sort of thing you might expect to get in a school cafeteria on a lot of planets."[13]

Such remarks wouldn't be nearly as effective coming from a hypercritical teenager or from a worldly-wise adult. The openness of these pre-adolescent characters to new experiences, and their lack of practice at rushing to assumptions and judgments lends authenticity to their droll recitals of the mayhem in Pinkwater's novels.

The device of telling a story through a naïve young observer has been employed with fine comic and satirical effect in many revered novels, among them Voltaire's *Candide,* Fielding's *Tom Jones,* and Twain's *Huckleberry Finn.*[14] The sophisticated reader is engaged by opportunities to read between and beyond the lines of the protagonist's limited understanding of his own experiences. Daniel Pinkwater's novels, which share some of the picaresque qualities of the aforementioned classics, make excellent use of this device.

One of the most notable characteristics of Pinkwater's shorter middle-grade books is his frequent use of food-related themes: types of food, varied dining establishments and eating habits, the vice of gluttony, and the consequence of obesity. These elements are prevalent in all of Pinkwater's writings, but nowhere does he mine them more intensively than in his short middle-grade works. The very title, *Fat Men From Space*, conveys the centrality of food and fatness in that story, whose premise is the invasion of Earth by pudgy aliens intent upon the consumption of all the planet's junk food. *Slaves of Spiegel*, essentially a sequel to *Fat Men From Space*, continues the story of these fat space pirates, as they organize an intergalactic competition to have the most excessive junk food banquet ever known prepared for them.

Both of the earlier entries in the Magic Moscow trilogy include similar scenes of outrageous gluttony. Again, there is a bizarre mingling of junk food and health food concepts, as in this passage from *The Magic Moscow*.

> The Moron's Delight is one of Steve's specialties. It has six flavors of ice cream—two scoops of each—a banana, a carrot, three kinds of syrup, whole roasted peanuts, a slice of swiss cheese, a radish, yogurt, wheat germ, and a kosher pickle. It is served in a shoebox lined with plastic wrap. Steve considers it a health-food dessert.[15]

Steve's other specialties, the Nuclear Meltdown and the Day of Wrath, also combine huge ice cream sundaes with vegetables, relishes, and other unlikely ingredients. The humor deriving from these scenes of fantastic excess follows a venerable literary tradition famously employed by Rabelais, and often found in American tall tales such as the frontier legends of Paul Bunyan, Davy Crockett, and Pecos Bill.

The Last Guru offers its own unique elaboration upon the theme of mixing fast and junk foods with health food. McTavish's, an imaginary health food version of McDonald's, is central to the story. The outlet features "french fried turnips, and carrot, celery, and pumpkin flavored milkshakes" as well as the Zenburger, a sandwich whose vegetarian patty is derived from pickles.[16] The adventurous approach to food expressed in these stories is ultimately carried on into the young adult novels, each of which includes scenes of gastronomical outrageousness.[17] *The Last Guru* anticipates the satire of both food faddishness and American misappropriations of Zen Buddhism that will figure in the young adult story, *Dead End Dada*.

Indeed, all of Pinkwater's intermediate fiction contains elements that can be found in his expedition novels and young adult novels as well. *The Hoboken Chicken Emergency* has numerous similarities to the two Snarkout novels, not least a fascination with unusual chickens. (*Hoboken*'s giant chicken, Henrietta, a.k.a. "Dirty Louise," is equaled by Dharmawati, the talented performing chicken of *Avocado*.) *Baconburg*, like *Hoboken*, is based upon the premise that a monster is on the loose. In both stories, silly newspaper reporters and fraudulent "experts" are attracted by the local hysteria, and absurd efforts to trap the "monster" merely heighten the pandemonium. Wild romps through lively urban neighborhoods at all hours provide adventure and excitement.

Also in the mode of the Snarkout novels is the affectionate relationship of *Hoboken*'s Arthur Bobowicz with his rather likeable parents. In Pinkwater's intermediate and young adult works, portrayals of such amiable family relationships are uncommon. In a number of these books the young characters are at odds with their parents. In others, particularly in the four expedition novels, the story takes place while the narrator and his parents are temporarily separated by summer vacations.

Attila the Pun also shares features with both Snarkout adventures. The story's central premise, that of using magic spells to summon the spirit of a famous historical figure, is played out in scenes rather like the one in which *Baconburg*'s Lydia LaZonga attempts to exorcise that novel's werewolf. The nocturnal atmosphere of *Attila*, featuring impromptu gatherings of odd characters at all-night restaurants, is quite similar to the enjoyably spooky atmosphere of the Snarkout novels. The mystic seer Lamont Penumbra and the ghostly Attila each give narrator Norman Bleistift an initial scare, but like many of the characters in the Snarkout novels, they turn out to be quite harmless, and both become splendid late-night pizza companions. Of course, being a ghost, Attila is unable to eat. However, since he enjoys the smell of pizza (he notes that there was no pizza in the fifth century), his living friends thoughtfully buy Attila his own pizza to sniff.[18]

The overt science fiction content of *Fat Men From Space* and *Slaves of Spiegel* is taken up in only one of the young adult novels, *Alan Mendelsohn*. However, the absurdly commonplace alien spacemen of those stories are the product of a humorous technique that is skillfully developed in many of Pinkwater's books. The superhuman being who turns out to have unexpected weaknesses has been a rich character type at least since the mythology of the ancient Greeks, whose heroes, Titans, and gods often had feet of clay. Pinkwater makes good use of comically flawed monsters and aliens in many of his picture books: the silly and harmless vampire guys in *Wempires*, the blustering title character of *The Devil in the Drain*, and funny little Captain Lumpy Lugo of *Ned Feldman, Space Pirate*. The humor derives from the enormous contrast between one's natural expectations of an omnipotent super being, and the mundane character who appears instead. In this scene from *Fat Men in Space*, a boy abducted by a flying saucer nervously prepares to meet his captors:

> The spacemen weren't at all what William had expected. . . . William guessed that they weighed at least 350 pounds apiece. . . . All the spacemen were wearing plaid sport jackets, and dacron slacks. They had knitted neckties, and black-and-white shoes with thick rubber soles. They all had crew cuts and they all wore eyeglasses made of heavy black plastic.[19]

The same type of humor is employed in several of Pinkwater's young adult novels. *Alan Mendelsohn*'s Clarence Yojimbo, immediately after demonstrating himself to be an alien from Venus with supernatural powers, needs to scrounge a few dollars for gasoline from the boys. In the same novel, a dreaded invisible beast and a trio of alien pirates are disarmed by a simple gesture. The fearsome "Avocado of Death" in the novel for which it is named turns out to be somewhat less than advertised. However, according to the know-it-all detective Osgood Sigerson, only emanations from that giant avocado, or Alligatron, can prevent an alien invasion. So when the Alligatron is destroyed, there is consternation:

> "But that means every licensed realtor in America is a creature from outer space!" I shouted. "What are we going to do about it?"
> "Well," said Osgood Sigerson, the world's greatest detective, "I suppose we'll just have to live with it." [20]

Just as we managed to live with an invasion of plaid-suited fat men from space.

Before those same plaid-suited fat men abducted Steve Nickelson and Norman Bleistift to participate in the great cooking contest on the planet Spiegel, we had the opportunity to spend some time with Steve and Norman in the more prosaic locale of Hoboken, New Jersey. The first two entries in Pinkwater's Magic Moscow trilogy, *The Magic Moscow* and *Attila the Pun*, are very enjoyable little books. Each of the

Magic Moscow stories becomes a little wilder, culminating in the sublime craziness of *Slaves of Spiegel*:

> Giant ducks from a planet of unknown name are led through the street, each duck held by a stout chain in the hands of a powerful Spiegelian pirate. The crowd cheers. The ducks snarl and hiss. The pirate duck handlers control the fearsome beasts.[21]

The Magic Moscow contains no such fantasy or science fiction elements. The title is derived from the name of an ice cream and sandwich shop owned and operated by Steve Nickelson, with help from his young assistant, Norman Bleistift. Early in the story, Steve obtains a Malamute pup from the odious kennel operator, John Crisco. The sickly pup, Edward, grows to be a big, strong dog, and he eventually achieves a comical triumph over Crisco's notorious champion Malamute at the Hoboken Sled Dog Club's annual show.

The Magic Moscow features several character types who reoccur in Pinkwater's novels. The appropriately-named puppy mill operator, John Crisco, is one of the outstanding members of a rogue's gallery of Pinkwater con artists. Along with the equally greasy Anthony DePalma of *The Hoboken Chicken Emergency*, this pair of outrageous opportunists set the pattern for the bold con artists of Pinkwater's young adult fiction, among them Samuel Klugarsh of *Alan Mendelsohn* and John Holyrood of *Dada Boys in Collitch*. The bumbling Sherlock Holmesian behavior of *The Magic Moscow*'s Sergeant Schwartz of the Yukon is one of many Sherlock Holmes parodies in Pinkwater's work, of which the most extensive and notable is the character of Osgood Sigerson in both Snarkout novels.[22]

Pinkwater's very first short novel, *Wingman* (1975) is the last to be discussed here, because in several respects it is quite uncharacteristic of the author's illustrated stories for pre-adolescents. This extraordinary story of a Chinese boy's triumph over racial and cultural discrimination in a New York public school, helped by a caring Caucasian teacher, is perhaps the most serious and straightforward of all Pinkwater's books. It is a heartwarming tale, and uniquely among Pinkwater's books, it contains very little humor. The illustrations are also special: nearly all of them are four-panel cartoons, in homage to the importance of comic books in the story.[23]

The protagonist, Donald Chen, is the usual pre-adolescent boy, and like many of Pinkwater's middle-grade protagonists he is in most respects a rather ordinary youth. But circumstances have made him an outsider: both "the only Chinese kid in Public School 132"[24] and obviously from a very poor home. Donald hadn't realized that he was so much worse off than his fellow students until the day he was ashamed to be singled out as one of the "poor" children in his class to be presented a filled Thanksgiving basket in front of his peers.[25]

Wingman is discussed at considerable length in the chapter on "First Novels" for young readers in Michele Landsberg's excellent book, *Reading For the Love of It*. Landsberg observes that, judging by their choices of fiction, pre-adolescent boys seem to long for

> the warmth and acceptance of a loving, all-powerful father without the competitiveness, the authoritarianism, and the harsh judging to which so many fathers are prone. In some versions, it is not the real-life father who is rejecting or inadequate, but society, in the guise of school authorities.
>
> *Wingman*, by Daniel Manus Pinkwater, seems to me to rank among the most beautiful and satisfying of all these fantasies.[26]

Landsberg confers high praise upon the text and illustrations of *Wingman*. She especially admires Pinkwater's ability to anchor a fantasy in tangible, carefully selected details of a young protagonist's everyday life.

> One of the great pleasures of Pinkwater is the way he can write obliquely, but with complete clarity of meaning. When he tells us that Donald goes to school every day, even in the coldest weather, without a coat but with a fresh white shirt, we know two things without being told: that his father anxiously looks after him in the only ways available to him (the clean white shirt is lovingly washed and ironed, of course, by the exhausted father), and that Donald is impervious to cold because he is numb with misery. Where lesser authors might have hammered home these perceptions in flat, declarative sentences, a true writer of fiction like Pinkwater tells us all by telling us practically nothing and letting it reverberate.[27]

As an outsider, Donald's problems coping with bad teachers in a mediocre school are greatly magnified. The centrality of the public school experience in *Wingman* connects it more closely to the young adult novels, particularly to *The Education of Robert Nifkin*, than with any of Pinkwater's other illustrated stories. In a curious way, Pinkwater's very first short novel and his most recent novel are much alike: both are quite serious and realistic accounts of rescue from bad teachers, and salvation with the help of good teachers. *Nifkin* is far more humorous than *Wingman*, much longer, and of course Robert Nifkin is considerably older than Donald Chen. Nevertheless, the strong common elements of these two stories, written a quarter of a century apart, bear witness to the consistent vision Pinkwater has maintained throughout his long and productive writing career.

In the next chapter we will examine four of Pinkwater's novels that do not fit all of the usual criteria for being considered young adult novels. The narrators are pre-teens, and the special challenges of adolescence are not addressed. Yet, these are substantial novels for and about young people. During an exchange with this author, Daniel Pinkwater wrote as follows concerning three of them:

> On reflection, I . . . think that if the ones you've cited are young adult novels, [i.e., the half-dozen titles covered in chapters 5-10 of this book] then *Borgel, The Worms of Kukumlima,* and *Yobgorgle, Mystery Monster of Lake Ontario* are too. They're just as long, just as complex, and were written in just the same way with just the same concentration and attention. So . . . you don't have to write about them, but you have to include the above statement, more or less . . . in a box.[28]

But of course those wonderful books have to be written about! Along with *Lizard Music,* which has been grouped with them because of its similar length, as well as for a special reason to be explained in the next chapter, these four novels are among Pinkwater's very best. Whether we call them young adult novels, middle-grade novels, or anything else, they contain four fantastic expeditions

NOTES

1. Pinkwater also co-authored the middle-grade novel, *Java Jack* in 1980. (Keele, Luqman & Daniel Pinkwater, *Java Jack* [New York: Crowell, 1980].) However, that book is uncharacteristic of Pinkwater's work, and it will not be discussed here. Pinkwater explained, "I was really the editor, not the co-author of *Java Jack.*" Email from D. Pinkwater to W. Hogan, 17 November 1999.
2. Email from D. Pinkwater to W. Hogan, 17 November 1999.
3. Email from D. Pinkwater to W. Hogan, 18 November 1999.
4. *The Last Guru* is intermediate in length, being shorter than the four expedition novels, but somewhat longer than the other half dozen middle-grade books.
5. Statements here about illustrative content are based upon first hardcover editions. Some reprint editions of Pinkwater's books have omitted artwork that accompanied the originals. For example, one of the titles reprinted in *5 Novels,* *The Last Guru,* had ten illustrations originally, but the reprint has none.
6. The recent paperback reprint of *The Hoboken Chicken Emergency* is illustrated in a similar manner, but with new drawings by Jill Pinkwater. Daniel Pinkwater, *The Hoboken Chicken Emergency* (New York: Aladdin Paperbacks, 1999). Jill Pinkwater has been illustrating most of her husband's recent books.

7. When asked why *Slaves of Spiegel*, alone among the Magic Moscow trilogy (indeed, alone among all of his seven shorter middle grade books) was not illustrated, Pinkwater replied, "If there was a special reason, I don't remember it. I don't think there was ever any discussion or intention to illustrate it. It's a lot larger in scope than the first two Magic Moscow books, taking place outside Hoboken, and Steve and Norman's usual environs." Email from D. Pinkwater to W. Hogan, 6 March 2000.

8. When asked about the technique used for the illustrations of *Lizard Music*, Pinkwater responded, "I am not 100% sure, but as I remember, they were linoleum cuts. I made very few lino cuts, always preferring wood, and have no idea what would have prompted me to use lino." Email from D. Pinkwater to W. Hogan, 6 March 2000.

9. *Young Adults* contains cartoon sequences, but these are separate from the text.

10. The protagonists of the eleven middle grade stories cannot all be described as "narrators," because the first four of these works (*Wingman, Hoboken Chicken Emergency, Last Guru, Fat Men in Space*) are written in the third person, a technique common to Pinkwater's picture books, but not to his novels. All of Pinkwater's subsequent longer fiction has featured a first person narrator. *Slaves of Spiegel* and *The Snarkout Boys and the Baconburg Horror* present multiple narrative techniques, both first person and other.

11. Daniel Pinkwater, *Yobgorgle, Mystery Monster of Lake Ontario* (New York: Houghton Mifflin, 1979), 85; hereafter cited in text as *Yobgorgle*.

12. Daniel Pinkwater, *Slaves of Spiegel*. In Daniel Pinkwater, *5 Novels* (New York: Farrar, Strauss, Giroux, 1977), 295.

13. *Slaves of Speigel*, 357.

14. A famous example is Huckleberry Finn's comment, "If Emmeline Grangerford could make poetry like that before she was fourteen, there ain't no telling what she could 'a done by and by. Buck said she could rattle off poetry like nothing. She didn't ever have to stop to think." Mark Twain, *The Adventures of Huckleberry Finn* (New York: Random House, 1996), 146. The irony, of course, is Twain's, not Huck's.

15. Daniel Pinkwater, *The Magic Moscow* (New York: Scholastic, 1980), 20.

16. Daniel Pinkwater, *The Last Guru*. In Daniel Pinkwater, *5 Novels* (New York: Farrar, Strauss, Giroux, 1997), 488.

17. Pinkwater has reassured his fans, "Because of certain themes in my work, I am assumed by many to be a completely reckless eater—but it's not the case." *The (Sort of) Official Daniel Pinkwater Website, Talk to DP Forum, Archive p. 6* <http://www.designfoundry.com/p-zone> (1 March 2000).

18. Daniel Pinkwater, *Attila the Pun* (New York: Four Winds Press, 1981).

19. Daniel Pinkwater, *Fat Men From Space* (New York: Dell, 1977), 37.

20. Daniel Pinkwater, *The Snarkout Boys and the Avocado of Death* (New York: Lothrop, See & Shepard, 1982), 156; hereafter cited in text as *Avocado*.

21. *Slaves of Speigel*, 291.

22. Other extended Sherlock Holmes parodies by Pinkwater are developed in the picture books *The Muffin Fiend* and *The Moosepire*. Pinkwater's short story, *The Diary of a Ghurka Physician* is a priceless Holmes parody.

23. "Intended, presumably to evoke a comic-book format, the illustrations are kept from the danger of occasionally seeming amateurish by the snappy optical shading effects reminiscent of Roy Lichtenstein's work." Jane Geniesse, "Wingman," *New York Times Book Review* (4 May 1975): 40.

24. Daniel Pinkwater, *Wingman* (New York: Bantam, 1992), 1.

25. *Wingman*, 6.

26. Michelle Landsberg, *Reading For the Love of It* (New York: Prentice-Hall, 1986), 67.

27. Landsberg, 68.

28. Email from D. Pinkwater to W. Hogan, 17 November 1999.

Chapter 4

Four Expeditions

Among Daniel Pinkwater's books for the pre-adolescents, the four longest are *Lizard Music* (1976), *Yobgorgle, Mystery Monster of Lake Ontario* (1979), *The Worms of Kukumlima* (1981), and *Borgel* (1990). All are one hundred and fifty to one hundred and seventy pages in length—considerably longer than any of the seven works discussed in the previous chapter. All have recently been brought back into print. The earliest, *Lizard Music*,[1] was recently reprinted in a paperback edition. The latter three, along with *The Snarkout Boys and the Baconburg Horror*, comprise the contents of *4 Fantastic Novels*, published in summer, 2000.

These four longer novels for young readers have thematic similarities as well. Each centers upon an exotic journey, in which a young narrator goes off on an unusual expedition with one or more adults. In *Lizard Music*, Victor sets out onto Lake Mishagoo[2] with Charlie the Chicken Man. *Yobgorgle*'s Eugene Winkleman navigates Lake Ontario with his Uncle Mel and several other adults. Ronald Donald Almondotter is taken to Kukumlima, Africa by his grandfather, and Melvin Spellbound accompanies his "uncle" Borgel on an automobile trip into the unknown.

In each instance, the ultimate journey to an exotic, mysterious place is preceded by a preliminary journey. Victor first ventures alone from his suburb of McDonaldsville into the big city of Hogboro. After some preliminary adventures there, he departs with the Chicken Man for the Invisible Island of the lizards. Eugene first travels to Rochester with his Uncle Mel, then contacts Professor McFwain, and finally they all set out on Lake Ontario in search of Yobgorgle. Ronald insists upon working for his eccentric grandfather despite parental discouragement and as a result is invited to fly with him to Nairobi—an adventure already—before they further undertake a safari to locate the mysterious, hidden location of Kukumlima. Melvin is the only member of the Spellbound family who makes an effort to get to know their strange lodger, "uncle" Borgel. Eventually, Borgel invites him on a surprising journey. In each case, the narrator, a boy aged about ten or eleven, takes some initiative to become acquainted with an interesting, eccentric adult. And in all four novels, opportunities for adventurous expeditions follow from those relationships.

Moreover, the destination in each of these stories is a mysterious place or object that cannot be reached in any straightforward manner. The Invisible Island of the lizards, the "mystery monster" Yobgorgle, the uncharted land of Kukumlima, and Borgel's "alternate time-space continuum" are all phenomena normally inaccessible to the human senses.

An important clue to the nature of these locales or quest-objects is provided in the first of these novels, *Lizard Music*. Charlie the Chicken Man explains to Victor:

> Invisible Island has the quality of bending rays, such as rays of light. You know that light rays tend to travel in more or less straight lines, but they can be bent. Well, certain islands bend them a lot. If you look straight at Invisible Island, you don't see the island, you see *around* the island, and you think you're looking directly at whatever's on the other side. Also, if you sail straight at the island, you will simply sail around it, thinking you're going in a straight line. It isn't easy to explain—there's a book called *Mount Analogue* by René Daumal that tells all about it.[3]

Despite his modest disclaimer, Charlie has just given Victor a rather good little summary of a complex scientific theory which Daumal's character, Pierre Sogol, elaborates over a full nine pages—with the help of two diagrams—in the novel, *Mount Analogue*.[4] The general idea is that places may exist upon the earth, which due to their special physical properties, are hidden from normal observation. It is difficult, but not impossible, for any of us to find such a place. The island of Mount Analogue could be accessed from an area of the South Pacific, but entry is possible only via an invisible portal that does not open for everyone who sails by the location. A recent book-length study of Daumal's life and work included this explanation of the obstacles to locating the island of Mount Analogue:

> Because of the invisible closed shell of curvature that surrounds the island, it remains protected from human detection, but not always, not everywhere, and not for everyone. At a certain moment and in a certain place, certain persons (those who know and have a real wish to do so) can enter.[5]

Having finally reached the island, Daumal's travelers find that life there revolves around a single purpose: that of ascending the immensely tall mountain dominating its center. Everyone on the island is either a climber, a guide, or else a tradesman who has given up the climb and contented himself with provisioning the new expeditions. Aside from its considerable charm as a "marvel tale," the book is an allegory of man's quest for enlightenment. The book's full title is, *Mount Analogue; a Novel of Symbolically Authentic Non-Euclidian Adventures in Mountain Climbing*. Daumal himself was a mountaineer, and the metaphor of a great mountain as a pathway to knowledge came naturally to him. At its base, the mountain is anchored in the everyday world. But the mountain's summit, attainable only by the most dedicated seekers, rises above the clouds into the rarified air of spirituality.

Daumal's *Mount Analogue* is an important source not only for *Lizard Music*, as Pinkwater informed us through his character Charlie, but also for the other three novels discussed in this chapter. In addition it bears upon *Alan Mendelsohn, the Boy from Mars*, Pinkwater's first young adult novel. Michael Dirda, a perceptive and appreciative connoisseur of Pinkwater's books, recently noted this influence in his review of *5 Novels*.

> Pinkwater himself is more than just a clownman of Earth. Several of his novels—*The Worms of Kukumlima, Yobgorgle, Mystery Monster of Lake Ontario*—are partly based on the ideas of French philosophical novelist René Daumal, author of the cult classic *Mount-Analogue*.[6]

As we shall see, Daumal's short, unfinished book informs Pinkwater's "expedition novels" in a number of ways, and not only with respect to the quest for an elusive place or object. Perhaps most importantly, the generic identity of these Pinkwater novels is rather similar to that of *Mount Analogue*. In the introduction to his translation of *Mount Analogue*, Roger Shattuck notes,

> At the time of the book's appearance in France many reviewers speculated busily over the particular literary genre to which it should be assigned. Most of them settled for the *conte philosophique* in the tradition of Voltaire and Swift, crossed with the marvel tale in the tradition of Cyrano de Bergerac, Poe, and Jules Verne.[7]

Thus, *Mount Analogue* contains aspects of the philosophical novel, of which Voltaire's *Candide* and Swift's *Gulliver's Travels* are two famous examples.[8] At the same time, *Mount Analogue* also possesses elements of such Victorian "marvel tales" as Poe's *Descent Into the Maelstrom* and many of Jules Verne's novels, among them *Journey to the Center of the Earth, The Mysterious Island,* and *20,000 Leagues Under the Sea.*[9] In fact, the philosophical novel and the marvel tale have a great deal in common; both feature voyages to strange places, both are concerned more with ideas than with character development, and both genres include speculation on future or alternative societies and technologies. These qualities also characterize some of Daniel Pinkwater's novels, particularly the expedition novels discussed here.

When asked if *Mount Analogue* had made a strong impression on him, Pinkwater replied that a college teacher had given him the assignment of reading the book, then writing an ending for it. (The unfinished novel leaves off quite abruptly, in the middle of a sentence. It was the final work of Daumal, who died of tuberculosis in 1944 at the age of thirty-six.) Pinkwater continued:

> I read it with pleasure, but never handed in the paper, because writing an end to it was simply beyond me. I more or less forgot all about it. Quite possibly I have tried a couple of variations on the book, including an end, since then, and might do it again. . . . It's quite nice, don't you think? Numbers of kids have written to me that they managed to find a copy, not sure it was a real book until they held it in their hands. They all seemed to like it too.[10]

Pinkwater is quite right, *Mount Analogue* is a delightful book.[11] Let us examine each of Pinkwater's four long novels for preadolescents, with particular attention to the Daumalesque expedition upon which each is centered.

Lizard Music is one of Pinkwater's most highly-regarded novels. It won an American Library Association Notable Book award for 1976. The narrator is an eleven-year-old boy named Victor, whose last name is never stated. He is left alone for two weeks when his ditzy older sister, who was supposed to be taking care of him and the family home while their parents were away, goes off on a vacation with her friends. Victor begins seeing strange things on TV at night. He forms the impression that many of the people on TV are acting strangely, as if they were like the "pod people" from *Invasion of the Body Snatchers.* Then Victor discovers some unscheduled late night TV programming featuring large lizards who play musical instruments, talk on game shows, and do other surprising things.

Victor takes a bus to the nearby big city of Hogboro several times, and gets to know Charlie, an eccentric black man who carries about a performing chicken. Charlie pops up everywhere Victor goes, often disguised and using the names of semi-famous Renaissance painters as aliases. Finally, Charlie explains to Victor that the lizards who have been appearing on TV are real, and that they live on an invisible island in the large nearby lake. Charlie, Victor, and Charlie's chicken Claudia manage to get to the island by swimming under its invisible barrier. There they meet a population of intelligent lizards who have been watching the nearby humans on TV, and sometimes unintentionally projecting themselves to certain human viewers. Victor has some unique experiences on Invisible Island, including a climb to the summit and down into the crater of a mountain, and finally returns home. His sister and his parents come back from their respective vacations, and life returns to normal.

Victor's compulsion to visit Invisible Island is somewhat comparable to the obsession driving Roy Neary, the character played by Richard Dreyfuss in *Close Encounters of the Third Kind*, a notable film produced in the year following the publication of *Lizard Music*. An alien race is nearby, and a few humans are attuned to the clues and signals they give off. It is also similar to the impulse driving the characters of *Mount Analogue* to quest for that mysterious peak.

We have already noted the direct reference to Daumal's novel by Charlie, as an explanation of the physical properties of Invisible Island. Another feature *Lizard Music* shares with *Mount Analogue* is the notion that most people sleepwalk through their lives, as conveyed by the TV "pod people" of Pinkwater's novel, and by the townspeople of Daumal's island who live all their lives at the mountain's base without daring its ascent. Daumal, a disciple of Gurdjieff,[12] and Pinkwater, a student of Zen,[13] have in common an impulse toward transcendence.[14] That is, to the idea that there are higher truths beyond those normally accessible to our senses. Some discipline or training, usually more intensive than that of traditional religious observance, is needed to prepare the individual for receptivity to transcendental experience.

Yobgorgle, Mystery Monster of Lake Ontario has a somewhat similar premise to that of *Lizard Music*. It is narrated by Eugene Winkleman, a boy of about the same age as the earlier novel's Victor. Again, the parents leave on an extended vacation while their son is home for the summer. In this case, Eugene is under the supervision of his Uncle Mel. However, after his parents have departed, Uncle Mel finds that he has to spend two weeks in Rochester for a bit of in-service training on the latest developments in his profession, the junk food vending business. Eugene willingly accompanies him, and like Victor, he spends much of his time exploring a new city.

As Victor found Charlie the Chicken Man, Eugene finds his guide to adventure in the person of Professor Ambrose McFwain. The Professor is a wildly eccentric inventor and entrepreneur, as well as a seeker

50   Chapter 4

of Yobgorgle, an alleged Loch Ness-type monster of Lake Ontario. McFwain, Uncle Mel, and their new friend Colonel Ken Krenwinkle form a hilarious ensemble. Following a series of humorous episodes,[15] they venture together out onto Lake Ontario. During the night, they encounter the source of the Yobgorgle legend, the Flying Piggie ("*Deutsches Unterseeschwimmschweinboot Fliegendes Schwein*") a German submarine disguised as an enormous pink pig.[16] The seeming misnomer, "flying," turns out to be an apt reference both to "The Flying Dutchman" legend and to the submarine's imminent aerial adventure. Like the invisible island of the lizards, the Flying Piggie is compelled to drift throughout one of the Great Lakes, never getting close to land. The adventurers are allowed on board, where they find themselves captives of an irrational genius, much like Captain Nemo of Jules Verne's *20,000 Leagues Under the Sea*.

Just as Victor and Charlie had to employ the special method of swimming under the barrier of Invisible Island, Eugene and his friends must devise a strategy for returning to land. And as in the earlier novel, timing is critical because the Flying Piggie (like Lizard Island) would soon be moving farther from the shore. In *Yobgorgle*, the solution is to hydroplane above the water and effectively fly to land. All of the adventurers, including Captain Van Straaten of the Flying Piggie, make it to shore and all ends well.

The Worms of Kukumlima is yet another adventure involving a young male narrator aged ten or eleven, during his summer vacation. Ronald Donald Almondotter is taken by his grandfather to Africa. From Nairobi, they set out to find the uncharted place, Kukumlima, which according to a lost explorer's journal, is populated by intelligent extraterrestrial worms. Their safari has some remarkable similarities to Daumal's Mount Analogue expedition. A wise old African advises the travelers:

> In your search for Kukumlima, you must become lost. You must become lost within as well as without. . . . Only at the moment when not one of you is thinking about Kukumlima, or where you are, or where you are going—only then will you actually find Kukumlima.[17]

And so it transpires. The safari becomes lost, and all of the members are enjoying the moment and not worrying about their destination. Without any willed effort on their part, they are suddenly and unexpectedly led into Kukumlima. Like Mount Analogue, Kukumlima is not a feature of any map, and cannot be reached by any direct approach.[18] Like the Invisible Island of *Lizard Music*, Kukumlima features a volcanic crater. After having to surrender to fate in order to reach Kukumlima, paradoxically, the adventurers must exert considerable courage and ingenuity in order to escape from it. There is a coincidental volcanic eruption in the crater, much in the spirit of Jules Verne's *Journey to the Center of the Earth*, from which the explorers barely escape.[19]

The last of these expedition novels is *Borgel*. The narrator, Melvin Spellbound, is of course, "ten or eleven" years old.[20] Borgel is a strange old man who had talked his way into the Spellbound home several years earlier, vaguely describing himself as a distant relative of one side of the family or another ("Yours or your husband's—I'm not clear about which.") He claims to be one hundred and eleven years old, year after year (3).

Young Melvin gets to know Borgel, and is often invited to visit or join the old fellow. After a number of eccentric but perfectly realistic encounters, Borgel takes Melvin for a ride in his old jalopy, a "1937 Dorbzeldge sedan" (26). Before long, it becomes evident that the interstate highway has become an interstellar highway—an invisible vector of space—and that the Dorbzeldge is in effect functioning as a time machine and space ship.

As in many of Douglas Adams' novels,[21] outer space turns out to be populated by a very odd mixture of extraterrestrial creatures and locales, as well as some surprisingly familiar ones. A dreaded Grivnizoid ("something between an octopus and a gnarled oak tree . . . with eyestalks and really bad breath") (161) is found, disguised, at a rundown encampment known as Gypsy Bill's Resort and Spa and Hobo Camp and Junkyard. A hideous but amiable Anthropoid Bloboform operates an ordinary root beer stand.

Borgel explains that the journey is more an adventure in a parallel reality than one to a specific location elsewhere in the cosmos. At one point Borgel casually demonstrates the point by disappearing momentarily from a point they had seemingly traveled light years to reach, before quickly reappearing with some fig bars from his room at home! This startling disconnect demonstrates that Borgel and Melvin's voyage is to some extent a "mind trip" rather than a physical journey to a particular location. In its own way, *Borgel* is also in the spirit of Daumal's *Mount Analogue*, in which the goals of finding the island and climbing the mountain operate on both literal and metaphysical levels.

There are, of course, many tales in classical literature which can be appreciated both for the surface excitement of an adventure quest, and for deeper archetypal resonance. Homer's *Odyssey*, Bunyan's *Pilgrim's Progress*, the Grail legends, and Coleridge's *Rime of the Ancient Mariner* are but a few famous examples of vividly described physical journeys of great lyricism, in which extreme challenges of geography and climate form ideal settings for the allegorical tribulations of the travelers. In choosing marvelous expeditions as the basis for his longer novels for young readers, Pinkwater was tapping into a great literary tradition, filled with rich possibilities for good storytelling.

Although it is in these four expedition novels that Pinkwater made greatest use of the Daumalesque themes described here, he also carried them into the transitional novel *Alan Mendelsohn, the Boy from Mars*. That novel's characters are in junior high school, thus exactly midway in age between the ten-year-old narrators of the mid-grade novels and the high-school-aged characters of Pinkwater's young adult novels. *Alan Mendelsohn*, like the expedition novels, includes a science fiction journey to a parallel world which can only be accessed from an invisible portal in a special location. However, *Alan Mendelsohn* also features an emphasis upon the public school setting, and some other qualities we will examine, which are entirely characteristic of Pinkwater's young adult novels. Thus the expedition novels form a bridge between Pinkwater's novels for younger readers and his novels for adolescents, by means of an interesting transitional novel having qualities of both.

NOTES

1. Daniel Pinkwater, *Lizard Music* (New York: Dell Publishing, 1996).
2. "Lake Mishagoo" is presumably a variant of Lake Michigan, that Great Lake which borders Chicago, one of Pinkwater's childhood residences and the location of some of his stories, including *Robert Nifkin*. If so, *Lizard Music* and *Yobgorgle* each take place on one of the Great Lakes: Michigan and Ontario, respectively. However, *Lizard Music* is set in Hogboro, which from evidence in several of Pinkwater's books, must be located in the Hoboken, New Jersey area. This geographical anomaly is an interesting example of Pinkwater's tendency to blend recollections from three great metropolitan areas in which he resided during his early years: Los Angeles, Chicago, and New York City with its New Jersey environs. (Although in *Yobgorgle*, some of his characters insist that Los Angeles doesn't exist.)
3. *Lizard Music*, 101-02.
4. René Daumal, *Mount Analogue* (Boston: Shambhala, 1986). Translation and introduction by Roger Shattuck, 54-62.
5. Kathleen Ferrick Rosenblatt, *René Daumal: the Life and Work of a Mystic Guide* (Albany: SUNY Press, 1999), 203. [Nearly as cogent an explanation as that of Charlie the Chicken Man, n'est-ce pas?]
6. Michael Dirda, *Washington Post Book World* (7 September 1997): 1.
7. Roger Shattuck, his introduction to *Mount Analogue*, 21.
8. Also see discussion of Menippean satire in chapter 11.

9. Pinkwater responded to a fan who asked what authors influenced him, "As a kid, I soon moved on from such picture-books as were available and remember toiling through adventure novels, including Jules Verne, R.L. Stevenson, Dickens, Hugo—all made accessible by the precious Classics Comics, which one would read first, to get a general idea, and then tackle the book. We lost a fantastic resource when those stopped publication." *The (Sort of) Official Daniel Pinkwater Website, Talk to DP Forum, Archive,* 7 <*http://www. designfoundry.com/p-zone*> (10 November 1999)

10. Email from D. Pinkwater to W. Hogan, 11 February 2000.

11. Sadly, it can be hard to locate. The 1959 English translation by Roger Shattuck has been reprinted several times, but appears to have recently gone out of print again.

12. Georges Gurdjieff (b. 1872?, Alexandropol, Armenia, Russian Empire, d. October 29, 1949, Neuilly, near Paris) Greco-Armenian mystic and philosopher who founded an influential quasi-religious movement. *Encyclopedia Britannica Online* (15 March 2000).

13. Several of Pinkwater's stories, notably *The Last Guru* and *Dead End Dada,* feature extensive parodies of Western misappropriations of Zen philosophy. In one of his essays Pinkwater tells us, "I used to know all about Zen Buddhism. In fact, I was a sort of walking encyclopedia of Zen. I had read all the Zen books. I gave a report on Zen in a class in college, and got an A for it. At the drop of a hat, I would explain Zen to anyone who would listen." Daniel Pinkwater, *Hoboken Fish and Chicago Whistle* (Princeton, N.J.: Xlibris, 1999), 276.

14. Transcendence, from the Latin *transcendere* "to climb over"—thus literally applicable to the ascent of Mount Analogue and other such alpine challenges.

15. One of the funniest situations in *Yobgorgle* involves Col. Krenwinkle's hunting of vintage automobiles, the hoods of which are later mounted on the wall of his trophy room. That episode nicely complements Roger Zelazny's immortal short story, "Auto da Fe," about the fatal encounter of a legendary matador with a hostile Ford convertible. In *Dangerous Visions,* ed. Harlan Ellison (New York: Signet, 1967), 496-502.

16. Daniel Pinkwater, *Yobgorgle, Mystery Monster of Lake Ontario* (New York: Houghton Mifflin, 1979), 116.

17. Daniel Pinkwater, *The Worms of Kukumlima* (New York: Dutton, 1981), 69-70.

18. Series editor Patty Campbell reminded this author of another famous indirect approach: Lewis Carroll's *Through the Looking Glass* features a house which Alice can enter only by walking *away* from it.

19. Jules Verne, *Journey to the Center of the Earth,* 1864. The adventurers descend into a deep fissure in Iceland, and they are eventually spewed out of Mount Etna when that famous Sicilian volcano erupts.

20. Daniel Pinkwater, *Borgel* (New York: Macmillan, 1990), 7.

21. Similarities between some of Daniel Pinkwater's novels and those of Douglas Adams have been noted by a number of reviewers. Pinkwater (1941-) began publishing books with science fiction content in the early 1970s. Adams (1952-) gained immediate fame in 1979 with his bestselling first novel, *A*

Hitchhiker's Guide to the Galaxy. The following assertion by Adams could as easily—and as accurately—have been made by Pinkwater: "I'm not a science fiction writer, but a comedy writer who happens to be using the conventions of science fiction for this particular thing." *Contemporary Authors* (Detroit: Gale Research Co., 1982), vol. 106, 15.

Chapter 5

Alan Mendelsohn, the Boy from Mars

When *Alan Mendelsohn, the Boy from Mars* was published in 1979, it marked a breakthrough in Daniel Pinkwater's development as an author. At that time, he had been producing children's books for nearly a decade. However, none were as long as *Alan Mendelsohn*, which at 248 pages still remains by far Pinkwater's longest novel. The book was well-received by reviewers. In *Kliatt*, Fran Lantz said it was Pinkwater's "best book since *Lizard Music*. . . . It's terrific!" [1] The article naming *Alan Mendelsohn* as one of the ALA Best Books for Spring 1979 called the novel "A blast." [2] The *School Library Journal* article said "Pinkwater('s) . . . non-Euclidian vision leaves some readers limp with laughter and others glassy-eyed." [3] The review in *Childhood Education* described it as "A wonderfully zany story." [4] Several years later, Jack Lechner gave the book high praise in *The Village Voice Literary Supplement*: Calling *Alan Mendelsohn* "one of the best" of Pinkwater's 30+ books published through 1986, he went on to say, "AM has more than yuks—Pinkwater's grasp of the confusing realities of pre-puberty leaves Judy Blume and company in the dust. He evokes the swirling sensory world of Leonard Neeble's Hogboro . . . with rich precision. You don't just feel for the kid; you feel *like* the kid. Sensitivity, intelligence, an original comic mind—I was hooked." [5]

Alan Mendelsohn takes place in junior high school, thus the narrator and his peers are several years younger than the high-school-aged protagonists of the YA books to be discussed in the next four chapters. Moreover, *Alan Mendelsohn* does not deal with romance, sexuality, cars, alcohol, or other topics of particular relevance to older teens. Nevertheless, the novel clearly represents a transitional leap by Pinkwater from being an author of books for younger readers toward becoming an author of books written for and about adolescents.

Alan Mendelsohn demonstrated that Pinkwater could sustain a full-length comic novel. Nearly all comic/satirical artists—cartoonists, stand-up comedians, and writers—initially develop their craft by means of small, clever sketches. For most of them, it is a formidable challenge to carry their talents onto a larger stage, represented by the feature film or the full-length play or novel. *Alan Mendelsohn* is the book which showed that Pinkwater could deliver a successful longer work, with both length and content suited to more advanced readers. Although it has strong roots in the earlier mid-grade novels (Pinkwater himself told a reviewer that *Alan Mendelsohn* was "*Lizard Music* with twice as many words"),[6] in important ways the book is more than a long mid-grade novel. It marks Pinkwater's entry into the young adult scene.

The novel is narrated by Leonard Neeble, a twelve-year-old boy whose parents have recently decided to move from a shabby but lively old multiethnic neighborhood to the sterile suburb of West Kangaroo Park. The parents seem to be pleased with their duller and more prosperous new surroundings, and quickly settle in to the suburban lifestyle, enthused over their backyard barbecues, automatic garage door, and tacky redecorating projects. Leonard, however, is miserable. He's left behind a support system of friends, relatives, and familiar places. No time period is specified, but like many of Pinkwater's books, *Alan Mendelsohn* is saturated with the 1950s atmosphere of Pinkwater's own youth, rather than the late 1970s when the book was written.

Although he's unstimulated by his new neighborhood, and by his home life as the only child of dull parents, most of Leonard's misery centers around his experiences at Bat Masterton Junior High School. The centrality of school in *Alan Mendelsohn* is one of the clues that this novel may have more in common with Pinkwater's subsequent YA novels than with his books for intermediate readers. Only one of the eleven middle grade novels, *Wingman*, is centered upon the school experience.

Two other aspects of this novel place it with Pinkwater's other YA books. First, the realistic depth and details of Leonard's *angst*. Unlike the simpler, often naïve narrators of most of the mid-grade novels, Leonard experiences deep and complex feelings, rendered in considerable detail. He vividly conveys the unhappiness of an adolescent, or more precisely, an almost-adolescent outsider, and we feel his pain. Yet another important clue that this is a new kind of Pinkwater novel is the appearance of a "buddy." Unlike his previous books, in which the young narrators are usually surrounded by adults, all of Pinkwater's YA novels feature one or more peer companions whose company the protagonist prefers to that of adults: Winston and Rat in the Snarkout novels, the Wild Dada Ducks in *Young Adults*, and Kenny and Linda in *Robert Nifkin*.

The opening sentence of *Alan Mendelsohn*, "I got off to a bad start at Bat Masterton Junior High School"[7] turns out to be a major understatement. Leonard's "bad start" consists of an unrelieved series of painful indignities and humiliations, related in a low-key, understated style both pathetic and funny. He "didn't know a single kid at the school." He is "a short, portly kid" with wrinkled clothes and eyeglasses. "Every other kid in the school was tall, had a suntan, and none of them wore glasses" (3).

Each time he enters a classroom, the kids giggle at the sight of him, then when they hear his name, "Leonard Neeble" they "go wild" with laughter. Nobody talks to him. The gym teacher, Mr. Jerris, is brutal, and "the teachers seemed annoyed that I was there, making them sign one more thing or send for an extra textbook." By the time school lets out, he is "totally miserable. But when his mother asks," 'How do you like your new school?' he tells her "it was fine—what else could I say?" (7). Leonard's inability to share his misery with any family member or friend is a suitable ending to a depressing opening chapter about his first day in the new school.

Leonard's next day at Bat Masterton is hardly an improvement. In his homeroom, "a girl about six feet tall" evicts him from an unassigned desk, and when he tries to placate her, she responds viciously, "Just get out of here, you little pimple" (14). He introduces himself to another student, who replies, "Yeah, I know. . . . You're the weirdo" (16). In his first class, he is made to stand at the front of the room and tell about his summer vacation. Everything the teacher draws out of him causes him mortification in front of his classmates. The gym teacher screams at him, 'FATSO, WHERE ARE YOUR GYM SHOES?" (18). But, seeing that the boys are expected to demonstrate a high level of physical fitness, he soon decides "to leave my brand-new gym shoes at home in my closet for as long as possible" (19). After a few days Mr. Jerris ignores him and lets him sit in the bleachers all during gym class.[8] Leonard also acts "dumb" in his regular classes, and eventually all the teachers ignore him. Leonard has exchanged sharp pains for dull ones.

> The only trouble was, it was boring. If I brought something to read, the teachers might have caught on that I wasn't really stupid.
> . . . I used to wonder what would happen to a kid who really was as dumb as I was pretending to be. Nobody would help him, he would just sit there like I was doing. (20)

In fact, Leonard is an excellent reader. Aside from regular recreational reading, he goes through all of his textbooks within a couple of weeks, then listens, bemused, as the simplest reading assignments cause his classmates to "all go 'Awwwwww' as though they had just been asked to crawl ten miles on their hands and knees" (21). Of course, none of them volunteer to recite, and few are able to respond when asked about the assigned readings.

Leonard finds a few other outcast kids, "but they all wanted to be regular Bat Masterton kids. They didn't want to be seen with me or any of the other weirdos, and they kept trying to be accepted by the real kids." Leonard seems to be hitting rock bottom. His thoughts are black: "The other weird kids all hated me. . . . I used to spend time trying to pick the one who would be the lowest person in the school if I dropped dead" (21).

But then something happens. Chapter 5 opens with a new voice, which seems to be coming from "this kid I'd never seen before. 'Are you talking to me?' I asked. Nobody had talked to me for weeks" (24). The new kid is Alan Mendelsohn, and he and Leonard quickly become friends.

Alan is a fearless nonconformist. He shares Leonard's low opinion of the school, its teachers, administrators, and students. But unlike Leonard, Alan doesn't let any of it get him down. Alan cheerfully plays practical jokes on fellow students, such as emitting a piercing whistle at just the right moment to cause a hapless victim to trip or bump into something.[9]

Alan also takes a very different approach to Leonard's in coping with the dull classroom curriculum. Instead of pretending to be dumb, Alan flaunts his intelligence, reciting at every opportunity, and regaling the classes with "weird things about the subject that the teacher never knew" (27). He tells the class all about Benjamin Franklin's sex life, and when the teacher tries to squelch him, Alan brings in "all these books the next day to prove that everything he had to say was true." Alan is frequently sent to the principal's office, and soon he is even suspended from school for a week for claiming to be a Martian and starting a riot.

Although Leonard is much happier at school now that he has a friend, when report cards come out it is found that he is failing every course. But from this apparent disaster a number of lively results emerge. The guidance counselor, a former wood-shop teacher who tells Leonard he obtained his counseling credentials "from a correspondence school in Ohio," recommends a private child psychologist. Leonard is soon getting time off school for appointments with the wildly eccentric Dr. Prince, who is easily manipulated into prescribing a full week away from school to reduce Leonard's "anxiety." This is, of course, the week of Alan Mendelsohn's suspension, freeing the boys for several days of non-traditional education together.

We are treated to several of Leonard's visits to Dr. Prince, sometimes accompanied by Alan. When Leonard tells the psychiatrist about some of his actual experiences, Dr. Prince replies, "Leonard, I can't tell you how pleased I am that you trust me enough to share your psychotic fantasies with me. Now we'll really make some progress" (126). A few moments later, Dr. Prince follows the boys into the hallway. "Don't worry about a thing," he shouted down the hall as we headed for the elevator, "I've cured people twice as crazy as you" (127). Since all the office workers on the elevator have heard this, Leonard and Alan pull their legs by pretending aloud that Leonard has incurable leprosy, and everyone but the boys exits the elevator on the seventh floor (128).

During that week the pair have a number of enjoyable adventures. On their first expedition into Hogboro, they notice a tattoo parlor. "We discussed getting tattooed, but neither of us could find anything we absolutely would like to have on our skin. About the best one was Donald Duck, with the word *Mother* written underneath. We decided to give it more thought" (50). Soon, they discover the Bermuda Triangle Chili Parlor, which Leonard recommends to Dr. Prince. The psychiatrist throws a public tantrum when he finds that corn muffins are not available in the evening. Eventually he settles for chili. "Ah, Leonard," Dr. Prince said, "you must excuse my perturbed state a moment ago. I become unreasonable when I am denied gratification I have been anticipating" (133). It is evident that all his years of graduate education and clinical experience have taught Dr. Prince how to diagnose and articulate his own neuroses, but not how to behave like a mature adult.

A moment later, we are treated to Dr. Prince's first experience of Green Death Chili,[10] as his face turns bright red, he sweats profusely, and tears stream down his face. "Without a doubt, the best chili I've ever tasted," he declares, when he has downed several glasses of water and recovered sufficiently to speak. And his companion's casual reply, "Now, eat up. If you don't go into shock from the first spoonful it's clear sailing after that" (134).

The boys' most important experience during their visit to Hogboro is their encounter with Samuel Klugarsh, owner of an occult bookstore and peddler of "Mind Control" programs. Klugarsh persuades them to buy some extremely phony-looking manuals and paraphernalia which will supposedly enable users to develop paranormal skills. To the surprise of the boys, the book's readers, and Klugarsh himself, the techniques work.

When they return to school after their week off, Leonard and Alan practice little mind-control pranks on their fellow students. Interestingly, the boys, who are social outcasts, seem to have no interest in

using their powers to gain popularity. They are content to remain outsiders and to perform their sabotage without calling any attention to
themselves. They concede that having an audience would be more fun,
but they continue to take care not to allow themselves to be identified
as the authors of their numerous pranks. When they use their new
mental powers to cause all the school clocks to run twenty-two minutes
fast one afternoon, they make a point of arriving at school late the next
morning like all the other kids "so as not to arouse suspicion" (121).

Nevertheless, the exercise of these new powers is subtly working a
change in Leonard. For the first time, he is gaining some control of his
environment, and he is no longer simply a passive victim. What is essential is that he is beginning to feel better about himself, even though
no improvements have yet occurred in his environment.

At the end of a week of pranks, the boys have their greatest adventure, the Saturday excursion to "another existential plane," after
which Alan disappears as suddenly and mysteriously as he had arrived
in Leonard's life. When Leonard returns to school without Alan, he
now emerges from his shell and begins acting exactly as Alan Mendelsohn had done: reciting frequently, and flaunting both his knowledge
and his individuality. Leonard's daring behavior brings about good
results: he assertively confronts his brutish gym teacher and secures
reassignment to an "alternative gym class" which he enjoys, he makes
friends in school, and he becomes an "A" student.

What has happened to change Leonard's outlook and behavior?
Except for the alternative gym class, Bat Masterton Junior High is the
same place that had driven him into deep depression. And his only
friend has gone. But Leonard has decided he is not going to let it de-
stroy him. He's going to thrive and to enjoy his life no matter how bad
the school is. He has come alive, and he now has the courage to be
himself. He still doesn't fit in, he still dislikes the school, but he's no
longer in shock, and he's able to function. He's not going to let the
place distort his personality or muzzle him. He still refuses to conform
to the expectations of either his teachers or his schoolmates. However,
he no longer feels that he must suppress his own natural abilities. He
realizes that following an "antiscript," i.e., having a knee-jerk negative
response, is just another way of being controlled by others. Since Leonard has all the tools to be an excellent student, he will be one, even if
his lively mind is out of synch with the intellectually stagnant environment of Bat Masterton Junior High, its teachers, students, and curriculum.

The progression that Leonard makes from lonely and depressed
outcast to a self-confident young man is a journey that many young

people must make. It is a very real story, albeit dressed up with comedy and science fiction, of an early adolescent beginning to come into his own. The importance of a close friend is genuine, even if that friend happens to be a "Martian." The boys' adventures in the lost world of Waka-Waka, at first glance an excursion in pure science fiction absurdity along the lines of *Slaves of Spiegel* or *Fat Men From Space*, in fact show us exactly what has happened to Leonard. The episode neatly parallels the action taking place in Leonard's real world. The apathy of the Waka-Wakians—their depression, their total subservience to the Nafuslian pirates, and their dread of the harmless "Wozzle"—is a parable of Leonard's situation at Bat Masterton Junior High. Again, Alan Mendelsohn shows what needs to be done. Following his friend's daring leadership, Leonard helps Alan to defeat the pirates and save the populace from oppression. This experience in taking assertive action carries over, and serves Leonard well when he returns to school. The episode also illustrates that conformity and fear are not issues for teenagers alone: adults, here the Waka-Wakian populace, sometimes face the same kinds of problems. In school, in the adult world, and perhaps even on other worlds (!) there are individuals and groups who try to maintain domination over others by keeping their subjects ignorant, docile, and subservient. One may need to summon some chutzpah to fight against such passivity, even if nobody else seems to care.

Of course, the boys' victory over the pirates is presented comically. One of the first mind control tricks they mastered was that of compelling a subject to simultaneously pat his stomach and remove his hat. The novelty of that exercise quickly wore off and was almost forgotten as the boys moved on to more meaningful techniques. Then, at the climax of the story, Alan and Leonard are told that by an extraordinary coincidence, this ridiculous double movement is precisely "the ultimate Nafsulian gesture of surrender, which no Nafsulian can retract" (216). Naturally, the boys execute their little trick on the Nafsulian pirates and so save an entire planet from tyranny.

In his Afterword to the novel, Pinkwater tells us: "*Alan Mendelsohn, the Boy from Mars* . . . is a compilation of more or less factual incidents, with a sort of blueprint for insurrection included to hold the reader's interest."[11] This remark provides a valuable key to what is going on in *Alan Mendelsohn* and in many of Pinkwater's other books. Smart, creative young people often find themselves stuck in dull, conformist schools. It can be an unpleasant, soul-destroying experience if one doesn't find a way of coping. Pinkwater is telling them: Don't despair because the teachers are time-passers and many of the kids shallow, lazy conformists who only care about appearances. It's more important to save your integrity than to be like everyone else and gain acceptance. The path of least resistance may seem inviting at the moment, but over the long run, one will regret not having been true to oneself.

"Insurrection" is not held up as a value for it's own sake; rather, it is something that may be necessary in order to maintain one's sense of humor, selfhood, and integrity in the face of formidable authoritarian and societal pressures to conform to the cookie cutter. In any case, for a "nerd" who doesn't have the option to be a popular kid, there is little to lose. If most of your schoolmates aren't going to like you anyway—simply because you don't look like a football star or cheerleader—why not be yourself, let loose, and give full expression to your uniqueness and individuality. To paraphrase Matthew xvi:26, "What is a child profited, if he shall gain junior high school popularity, and lose his own soul?"

Like many of Pinkwater's young protagonists, Leonard is aided by a charismatic figure who leads him on adventures that give him hope and teach him important techniques in self-reliance. The charismatic leader in this novel, Alan Mendelsohn, represents an interesting variation on this character type in Pinkwater's fiction. Most of Alan's behavior is that of an ordinary young adolescent, and in this respect Alan is simply a "buddy" like Winston Bongo in the Snarkout novels. However, in view of Alan's role in rescuing Leonard, a more apt comparison might be to Kenny Papescu from *The Education of Robert Nifkin*. As we shall see, that novel is in many respects a remake of *Alan Mendelsohn*, twenty years later, for older readers.

However, in other respects, Alan is more like the fantastic Wingman from the novel of that name, or like *Lizard Music*'s Charlie the Chicken Man. That is, to the extent that he is a "Martian," and in view of his convenient appearance and disappearance, Alan functions as a "Deus ex machina" character. He is dropped into the novel and then whisked out of it when no longer needed, as fortuitously as Jupiter being lowered and raised from the Elizabethan stage, or as the Fairy Godmother's appearances and disappearances from *Cinderella*.

In *Wingman*, Donald Chen is inspired and saved by two characters: the fantastic Wingman, and the very real substitute teacher, Mrs. Miller. In *Alan Mendelsohn*, the two characters who play those roles in Leonard's life are embodied in one and the same person: Alan Mendelsohn the Martian and Alan Mendelsohn the real boy.

When he helps Alan Mendelsohn to defeat the Nafsulian pirates, and when he returns to school and carves out a place for himself at Bat

Masterton Junior High, Leonard finds that there is no simple script for mastering life's challenges. Success is not guaranteed by any formal code of behavior. The boys must be creative to figure out how to defeat the Nafsulian pirates, just as Leonard has to be imaginative and resourceful to find his way in the real world. A number of reviewers have noted the "street smarts" of Pinkwater's heroes, for example Jack Lechner noted, "Most of the protagonists [in Pinkwater's books] are a lot like Leonard Neeble: smart, resourceful kids, ready to handle anything." [12]

Sometimes resourcefulness involves bending a few rules. Pinkwater's books also display a fascination with con artists, hucksters, mountebanks, and imposters. In *Alan Mendelsohn*, Pinkwater warms up to his theme by first presenting a number of adult characters who are merely incompetent: Leonard's parents for starters, then the entire staff of Bat Masterton Junior High, including, for example, Mr. Heinz, who had been the wood-shop instructor, but switched to guidance counselor when the school needed one, for which he became qualified by taking a correspondence course from Dr. Prince. Dr. Prince himself, not an especially talented psychologist. Bookseller William Lloyd Floyd, whose idea of writing a literary masterpiece is to type every word he hears spoken.

Eventually the boys meet Manny, Moe, and Jack, [13] the Nafsulian pirates who have pulled a giant scam on the entire planet of Waka-Waka. However, the book's genuine con artist is Samuel Klugarsh, the fraud who peddles badly mimeographed manuals and shoddy training devices that he believes are of no real value. One reviewer said of Pinkwater's formula for fantasy,

> The power, or key to it, in each of his novels resides in some impotent adult, such as an over-the-hill, obvious con artist—Samuel Klugarsh is the latest one—whose fraud is so blatant that it can be topped only by the surprise of his actually having the power without even knowing it. [14]

There have been many variations on this theme in Pinkwater's books: the title character of *The Return of the Blue Moose*, who writes a dreadfully bad novel, refuses to allow any revisions, and then sees it become a bestseller. Professor Ambrose McFwain in *Yobgorgle* who is seeking a Loch Ness sort of monster in Lake Erie, and actually finds something. Mozart in *The Muffin Fiend*, and Sigerson in the Snarkout books, both pompous detectives who solve their cases despite using absurd methods. Pilots Roosman and Rassman of *The Worms of Kukumlima*, who "cheer wildly" upon landing their plane safely in Nairobi, after flying the Atlantic by dead reckoning. Braggarts and poseurs who seem totally out of their depth, and then somehow succeed—sometimes to their own surprise, always to ours—and often not according to plan.

Pinkwater gets double duty from these situations. The initial comedy derives from recognition of the ridiculously insincere and/or inept con artist, and the absurd naïveté of the characters in the story who put their trust in him. Then while the reader is still laughing at the initial preposterous situation, a second stage of silliness unfolds as it becomes evident that the bumbling con artist is really on to something despite himself.

These inauthentic and insincere con men have provided plenty of humor in Pinkwater's fiction. However, they also play an important role in allowing Pinkwater to express some deeply-held beliefs through his stories. Such characters, and the situations they get into, provide the author opportunities to illustrate his disdain for authoritarianism and conformity, and for the need to resist them. Conning and cunning are appropriate responses to excessively rigid rules.

In Pinkwater's fictional world, there are too many rules and too many authority figures limiting the creative imagination and the flourishing of the individual personality. Various characters, both heroes and rascals, rebel against these constrictions. In several of his stories, including *Alan Mendelsohn*, the boy protagonists must become con artists in their own way, trying to outwit parents, teachers, and other authority figures. Leonard cons Dr. Prince into giving him a week off school. Alan plays pranks on teachers and classmates, and Leonard eventually joins in these activities. In contrast to the apathetic Waka-Wakians, the boys are able to plan and execute a clever plan to defeat the pirates and their Wozzle. Klugarsh tries to con the boys, but he is an ineffectual trickster, and the boys get the better of the deal. Klugarsh himself becomes an object of ridicule. The Venusian, Clarence Yojimbo, proves his psychic powers by telling Samuel Klugarsh (and numerous others within hearing) what sort of undershorts Klugarsh is wearing: "blue with white stripes" (137) the first time they meet, and "white with little red hearts on them" the next (151).

In Pinkwater's YA novels, a benevolent sort of con artistry, a mischievous flim-flamming, is pervasive. It certainly gives rise to many comic situations, but it is also a key element of Pinkwater's "blueprint for insurrection." Moreover, it places Pinkwater's fiction in the mainstream of American literature. The gallery of colorful rascals and hustlers encountered by Leonard and Alan brings to mind the rogues of such picaresque American novels as *Huckleberry Finn* and *Catch-22*.

In these rambling novels, young protagonists have to find their way past numerous absurd situations and self-serving con artists. Survival in such a topsy-turvy world requires learning how to break a few rules and out-hustle the hustlers, preferably without becoming entirely cynical and losing one's basic goodness. The protagonist must learn a few tricks, not because he enjoys victimizing others, but simply in order to survive.[15] "Mind-control techniques" are a metaphor for gaining control: first control of oneself—self-mastery; and then for learning to master problems of the external world.

With the publication of *Alan Mendelsohn, the Boy from Mars* in 1979, Pinkwater completed his first decade as an author with a well-received novel, much longer than any of his earlier books, and one which began to bring him to the attention of the older teen audience. In the following decade, he would go on to publish four more books for young adults.

NOTES

1. Fran Lantz, "Fiction: *Alan Mendelsohn, the Boy from Mars*" in *Kliatt Young Adult Paperback Book Guide* (September 1981): 14.
2. *School Library Journal* (May 1979): 36.
3. Patricia Manning, *School Library Journal* (May 1979): 66.
4. *Childhood Education* (January 1980): 169.
5. Jack Lechner, "Pinkwater Runs Deep," *Village Voice Literary Supplement* (March 1986): 18.
6. Ann S. Haskell, "The Fantastic Mr. Pinkwater." *New York Times Book Review* (29 April 1979): 32.
7. Daniel Pinkwater, *Alan Mendelsohn, the Boy from Mars* (New York: Dutton, 1979), 3; hereafter cited in text as *Alan Mendelsohn*.
8. The other boys spend most of their time climbing ropes. Leonard observes of a classmate, "He was Mr. Jerris's favorite kid. He could climb those ropes just like a cockroach." *Alan Mendelsohn*, 116.
9. This trick was famously displayed in Jacques Tati's 1957 film *Mon Oncle/My Uncle*, in which the delightfully nonconformist uncle played a role in his nephew's life very much like Alan Mendelsohn's role in Leonard's.
10. When asked for the recipe for Green Death Chili, Pinkwater replied, "I am enjoined by federal statute against sending the recipe for green death chili over the internet, on phone lines, or though the mail. It is also against the law to write it down, speak it, communicate it through signs, gestures, diagrams or rebuses, except in the state of Tennessee, where it can be scratched in the dirt with a stick, in the presence of adults without criminal records, provided it is rubbed out again at once." *The (Sort of) Official Daniel Pinkwater Website, Talk to DP Forum, Archive*, 2 <http://www.designfoundry.com/p-zone> (4 September 1999).

11. *Alan Mendelsohn*, [250].
12. Lechner, 18.
13. With an apology to The Pep Boys.
14. Haskell, 32.
15. Pinkwater's character, Robert Nifkin discusses the virtues of creative problem solving: "I once commented to Kenny that I could, theoretically, pass courses by doing work, and get a driver's license by learning how to drive first and then taking the test. Kenny said it was his opinion that I thought that way because I hadn't been brought up in Chicago. He said that doing things the regular way was uncreative and might become a habit in later life." Daniel Pinkwater, *The Education of Robert Nifkin* (New York: Farrar, Strauss & Giroux), 142.

Chapter 6

The Snarkout Boys and the Avocado of Death

During the years 1979-1982, in which his first YA novels appeared, Pinkwater also published half a dozen novels for younger readers: *Yobgorgle, Mystery Monster of Lake Ontario* (1979), *Java Jack* (1980), *The Worms of Kukumlima* (1981), and the complete Magic Moscow trilogy: *Magic Moscow* (1980), *Attila the Pun* (1981) and *Slaves of Spiegel* (1982).

Surprisingly, this extraordinary burst of mid-grade novels, like the grand finale of a fireworks display, marked the end of that phase of Pinkwater's writing career. During the eighteen years since 1982, he has published only one additional novel for the pre-adolescent audience, *Borgel*, in 1990. Although the great majority of Pinkwater's titles since 1982 have been picture books for young children, that year also saw the publication of two extraordinary young adult novels: *The Snarkout Boys and the Avocado of Death*, and *Young Adult Novel*. Each of these very different books was followed a few years later by a sequel: the former by *The Snarkout Boys and the Baconburg Horror* (1984), and the latter by *Young Adults* (1985).

Although Pinkwater had not been involved with formula series until quite recently, he has written a number of excellent sequels. In addition to the two pairs of YA novels and the Magic Moscow trilogy just mentioned, his long picture books about the Blue Moose are favorites: *The Blue Moose* (1975), *Return of the Moose* (1979), and *The Moosepire* (1986). There are also two "Kevin Spoon and Mason Mintz" picture books, *Doodle Flute* (1991), and *Spaceburger* (1993). Among Pinkwater's novel sequences, undoubtedly the most famous is the Snarkout duo, to which we will turn in this chapter and the next.

There are two interesting points to be made about the contemporary reviews of Pinkwater's second YA novel, *The Snarkout Boys and the Avocado of Death*. To begin with, several of the reviews were devoted to simultaneous coverage of three more of Pinkwater's new books, since he was so prolific around 1982. More importantly, the reviews of *Avocado* were not, on balance, especially favorable. This is surprising in retrospect, since the book is now considered a classic by most devotees of Pinkwater's fiction. *Avocado* was one of the titles selected for inclusion in the first Pinkwater omnibus, *5 Novels* (1997), and the paperback version has been in print almost continuously since 1983. Numerous reviewers of *The Snarkout Boys and the Baconburg Horror* (1984) praised *Avocado* while reviewing its sequel. There have been occasional rumors of a third Snarkout title, and *I Snarked With a Zombie* was announced in *Books in Print* during 1999. However, Daniel Pinkwater informed this author that there is no such book on his horizon.[1]

The negative reviews compared *Avocado* unfavorably with some of Pinkwater's earlier books. Robert Unsworth wrote for *School Library Journal* that the novel was "not up to the quality of his *Alan Mendelsohn*."[2] Kirkus Reviews concluded, "this is mainly random silliness without the inspired absurdity of *Lizard Music* and *Alan Mendelsohn* or even the buildups and comic eruptions of *Yobgorgle* and *The Worms of Kukumlima*."[3] Peter Andrews wrote a substantial essay in *The New York Times* covering *Slaves of Spiegel, Young Adult Novel,* and *Avocado*.[4] Andrews wrote that he liked "about one out of every three Pinkwater books," and that "the current triptych of novels by Mr. Pinkwater is a truly representative sampling." Andrews loved the first and hated the latter two books. We will be revisiting his important and influential review later in this chapter, and again in the discussion of *Young Adult Novel* in chapter 8.

There were also several mixed reviews. *Horn Book*: "The plot unfolds in a kind of verbal animated cartoon which might be just as successfully shown backwards as forwards. At times the humor is forced and the shenanigans laboriously outrageous, but there are some genuinely funny moments." The review concludes, "The book is not for the fainthearted nor for those looking for a reasonable plot, lyric prose, or convincing characters; it strains the reason, but the occasional nuggets of humor are worth the panning."[5] *Booklist*: "The plot line is lost at times in prolific Pinkwater's zany shenanigans, but the nonstop craziness is once again on target for a reader looking for the offbeat. This should tap new fans from a slightly older audience."[6] *Children's Book Review Service*: "If you're looking for a strange science-fiction book, then Daniel Pinkwater's book is just for you. . . . This weird book is not for your avid reader of mysteries. He or she needs to be a science-fiction lover to get through the book."[7]

There were some entirely positive notices. A "Trade News" article in *Publisher's Weekly* emphasized the author's remarkable productivity, and discussed the same four books that were reviewed by the New York Times: *Roger's Umbrella, Slaves of Spiegel, Young Adult Novel,* and *Avocado.*[8] As a trade publication, *Publisher's Weekly* is dedicated to promotion rather than criticism, but the article contains some interesting information; for example, the four new titles by Pinkwater in the spring of 1982 are "from four different publishers—an impressive total even in the prolific world of children's books." The reviews in *Voice of Youth Advocates* and *Kliatt Young Adult Paperback Guide* were altogether favorable. The former asserted that "Pinkwater's latest walk on the weird side is not likely to disappoint,"[9] and the latter described *Avocado* as "one of the author's better efforts. . . . There are a lot of laughs in this book, not to mention adventure, action and a real sense of wonder. A treat!"[10] But overall, the contemporary reviewers gave the book a mixed reception, at best.

Although numerous reviewers have characterized *Avocado* as a sprawling, rambling, wild and crazy story, the plot is not really so complicated. The narrator is Walter Galt, who has just begun his first year at Genghis Khan High School. In the opening pages he tells us about his parents, his home life, and his school. Soon we learn about "snarking," which involves sneaking out at night with his best friend Winston Bongo, and attending all-night movies at the Snark Theatre. When Winston catches German measles, Walter carries out his first solo snark and meets Rat, an unconventional girl who attends another local high school and also snarks. Winston soon recovers, and the boys get to know Rat and her eccentric family. When Rat's Uncle Flipping (said to be a mad scientist) mysteriously disappears, the three friends plan to search for him during their spring break.

The second half of *Avocado* (a bit larger than half, so it must be the side with the pit) consists of two consecutive evenings of adventure. On the first evening, Walter, Winston, and Rat begin at the Snark, then proceed to discover the richness of nightlife in the city's funky, bohemian "underworld." They meet a number of colorful characters, most importantly the detective Osgood Sigerson and his companion Dr. Ormond Sacker,[11] who are also looking for Uncle Flipping. They join forces and discover some important clues, including the location where the archvillain Wallace Nussbaum—purportedly aided by a brainwashed orangutan—is believed to be holding Uncle Flipping prisoner in order to gain control of a powerful invention: the "Avocado of Death," also known as the Alligatron. On the second evening, Sigerson leads the three youths, Sacker, and Winston's uncle (a pro wrestler known as the Mighty Gorilla) on an expedition to rescue Flipping and thwart Nussbaum. A wild melee ensues, Flipping is rescued, and Nussbaum captured. When his disguise is removed, Nussbaum turns out to be Rat's butler, Heinz.[12]

That's it in a nutshell, or to borrow Mr. Galt's favorite metaphor, in an avocado skin. The novel abounds with crazy characters and farcical situations, and so it presents an appearance of chaos. However, when one takes a moment to trace the essential plot beneath all the surface zaniness, one can be found. Does the novel hold together and make sense at any level as a coherent work of art, or is it just a silly romp?

As we have seen, the reviewers strongly tended toward the latter opinion. Even the most favorable reviews, while praising *Avocado* for its richness of comedy and atmosphere, made no claims for the book having any sort of thematic unity. The mixed reviews were unanimous in condemning the book's alleged lack of "a reasonable plot."[13] Two of the most hostile reviewers agreed upon a dismissive term. *Avocado* is described as "150 pages of silliness,"[14] in one review, and another contains two such references: the review's opening sentence, "The title is indicative of the silliness quotient of Pinkwater's latest exercise in outlandish adventure" and later, "this is mainly random silliness."[15]

The most important negative review of *Avocado* appeared within Peter Andrews' full-page essay on three Pinkwater novels in *The New York Times Book Review*. Andrews' general view of Pinkwater is of an undisciplined and self-indulgent author who has his moments, but who frequently overreaches and falls flat. "All too often Mr. Pinkwater falls into such raptures of self-amusement I can scarcely make out his jokes amid the peals of his own laughter." Like the majority of *Avocado's* reviewers, Andrews found the novel tough going. He not only doesn't think it funny, but doesn't "even understand it."

> There are too many mishandled elements in the story. . . . Mr. Pinkwater tosses so many balls in the air that he eventually drops them all, and punctuated by gag lines that have nothing solid to bounce off, his tale sinks into disarray. [16]

Andrews' article is significant not only because of the prestige of *The New York Times*, but also because of the intellectual quality of the reviewer's arguments. Andrews is a professional writer bringing formidable analytical powers to bear upon his subject. His criticisms must be taken seriously. Here he provides an analysis of what he regards as one of Pinkwater's major faults:

> He sometimes falls into the trap of thinking that if you are writing nonsense you don't have to be logical. Logic is, perhaps, the only

rule there is to follow for writing good nonsense. What should be delightful confusion in Pinkwater stories is frequently just a muddle.[17]

Andrews goes on to contrast *Slaves of Spiegel*, which he finds to be a logically constructed novel, with *Avocado*. The two books display the same sort of surface zaniness of character and incident, but according to Andrews, the former "is a wonderfully funny, goofball science fiction story," while the latter is "confusing . . . a literary enigma the National Security Agency would have difficulty deciphering."[18]

Is it possible to defend *Avocado* from this barrage of criticism? Could it be that so many experienced reviewers were wrong? Could all of them have misread the novel and failed to notice that *Avocado* might be more than a bowl of guacamole? Well, perhaps. Let's dip in.

Something unusual, something not mentioned by any of the reviewers, is taking place in *Avocado* beneath its bumpy, wrinkled skin. There are numerous clues throughout the book, and ten passages containing such clues are listed below in order of appearance. The reader may find it amusing to see how many clues he or she needs to solve the mystery. It shouldn't be hard to make something of these clues even if one has not yet read *The Snarkout Boys and the Avocado of Death*.

1. My father had searched for Flipping Hades Terwilliger? I was learning quite a lot about him this morning. He appeared to have a much more interesting life than I had thought (68).
2. [Sigerson] had his whole face covered with some kind of white make-up, and his hair was painted on—maybe with shoe polish. He had the same sideburns as Basil [Rathbone] but they were paint (73).
3. Osgood Sigerson licked the tip of his finger and ran it around the inside of the pie plate, picking up avocado crumbs. Rat and Winston looked at one another without expression. I knew what they were thinking. My own father is an avocado addict, and I know how depressing it can be to deal with one (107).
4. Sure enough, Osgood Sigerson launched immediately into a long discussion of avocado pastries around the world. I felt right at home, but I could tell that Rat and Winston were suffering intensely (107).
5. It was just dawn when I got back to the apartment. My father was already awake, sitting in the breakfast nook, having a cup of tea. I had never known he was such an early riser (124).
6. "Aren't you going to eat that?" Osgood Sigerson asked, snatching the intact-except-for-one-bite raisin toast from my plate. . . . As a general rule, I don't eat raisin toast. I don't know anybody who does, except my father. Maybe it's a taste that goes with liking avocados (132).
7. Sacker: "the orangutan led me to the Sausage Center Building."
   Walter: "That's where my father works!" I shouted (139).

8. Sigerson adjusted his false nose (140).
9. My father keeps his collar buttons . . . in an old nose-putty can (147).
10. Sigerson seems to make it to the [avocado] convention only every other year, and somehow those years my father doesn't go. He goes to the Sausage Maker's Association convention instead, which takes place the same week (148).

When these passages are lined up together, it becomes obvious that Walter's father has been playing the role of Osgood Sigerson. It is also possible that Sigerson's companion, Dr. Ormond Sacker, is played by Walter's mother. Sacker, like Sigerson, is in heavy disguise. He wears "a wig made out of a dust mop," (109) and apparently sounds appropriately masculine. We are told early in the novel that Mrs. Galt has a strong voice: "If you were blind, or only knew my mother from talking to her on the telephone, you'd probably think she was about six feet tall . . . and maybe two hundred and fifty pounds in weight. It's her voice, and the way she talks. . . . Actually she's small" (10). Moreover, like Mr. Galt and Sigerson, Mrs. Galt and Sacker are never in the same place at the same time. Beyond that, there is no strong evidence for or against the notion that Mrs. Galt might be playing Sacker. However, Pinkwater once gave the following response to an email question from a fan who asked if Mr. Galt was Sigerson:

> Any reader is entitled to any conclusions. I don't have to comment, and may not even know. I will say this: In the Lifeline Theater production in Chicago, not only does Walter's father turn out to be Sigerson, but Mrs. Galt turns out to be Sacker. Few people comment on this aspect of that book.[19]

At this point, one might concede, "O.K., so Walter's father was going around impersonating a Sherlock Holmes sort of character called Sigerson. Cute. But that still doesn't redeem all of the book's silliness. That alone doesn't make sense out of a very bizarre novel." And one would be right to say so. But the Galt/Sigerson play-acting is not all that's going on beneath the skin of *Avocado*. In fact, several characters are engaged in a fairly elaborate, but not implausible hoax. And despite all the trappings of fantasy and science fiction, not a single unnatural, or even outrageously improbable event occurs in the story.

The orangutan alleged to have been enslaved by Wallace Nussbaum is never seen clearly, and does not exist. It is (very appropriately) impersonated by Winston's muscular Uncle, the "Mighty Gorilla." Walter describes it: "I saw a hideous shape. It was the size of a big man, as big as the Mighty Gorilla" (142). The "Alligatron," a supposedly awesome invention, is a prop, switched on by Mr. Galt when he proceeds in advance of the others. It is glimpsed briefly on that occasion then never seen again. All of the crazy characters are being play-acted by ordinary people. In short, this allegedly silly and nonsensical story is in fact one of the most realistic of all Pinkwater's novels. It is one of the few of his seventy-plus works of fiction in which every character is a normal human being and every incident is completely in accord with the laws of nature. This is no coincidence. It was carefully planned by an author who is perhaps not quite so undisciplined as the reviewers thought.

Avocado is related to such novels as John Fowles' *The Magus,* in which the protagonist and the reader are pulled into exotic adventures which turn out to have been arranged: arranged by persons who were willing to go to a great deal of trouble to put on a masque—a complex, partially-scripted drama—on the stage of the protagonist's everyday life.[20] In *Avocado,* Sigerson is unquestionably played by Mr. Galt, and Sacker probably by Mrs. Galt. Sigerson and Sacker claim to have encountered all sorts of fantastic characters and situations, but these are hearsay, alleged to have taken place "offstage." Heinz, Rat's "Chinese butler," plays Wallace Nussbaum.

A few other adults had to have been in on the hoax. Winston's uncle, the Mighty Gorilla, assists Sigerson and also impersonates the orangutan. This is not a difficult role for a professional wrestler. Captain Shep Nesterman, the "Chicken Man" of *Lizard Music,* is an amiable street character who undoubtedly enjoyed his small part in escorting the youths to Sigerson. "Mr. Gutzman," who briefly impersonates the character played by Sydney Greenstreet in *The Maltese Falcon,* was another recruit with a minor role. The "night watchman" who is found tied up in a warehouse is yet another bit player, perhaps a double role by Captain Nesterman or by the actor playing Gutzman.[21]

Rat's parents, Mr. and Mrs. Matthews, may be in on the joke since they not only go along with the idea of Uncle Flipping's mysterious disappearance, but also encourage the youths to search for him. Sigerson supports Mrs. Matthews' loony insistence that "all licensed real-estate brokers are extraterrestrials" (120). We learn that both of Walter's parents went to high school with Mrs. Matthews' brother Flipping, so Rat's parents may well be full conspirators with Walter's in staging the hoax. The adults might all be amateur thespians who performed plays together back in high school. The alternate explanation is that the Matthews' are so eccentric that they really thought that Uncle Flipping had been kidnapped by a criminal mastermind, and that the best way to rescue him would be to send their daughter and a couple of other young teenagers to wander the city's streets at night rather than calling the police.

Other elements of the story neatly support the hoax. Conveniently placed pineapples and bananas are said to be evidence of the orangutan's activities, as is a preposterous newspaper clipping produced by Sacker. An indistinct dark object alleged to be a stuffed Indian fruit bat is produced at opportune moments.

"Sigerson" stage manages the hoax on numerous key occasions. He announces that the night watchman, "bound hand and foot with what must have been a thousand feet of Scotch tape" is a victim of Nussbaum and prevents anyone from untying him. On both evenings, "Sigerson" (Mr. Galt) proceeds in advance of the others to complete his preparations. He shows off by correctly predicting events that are part of the hoax, such as the disappearance of Heinz. He controls the pace: he is relaxed when everyone else is concerned, then he suddenly stirs everyone up when he is ready to spring a new adventure on them. He calls off the first evening's adventure at a very unexpected moment, surprising the youths with his certainty that there will be no harm in waiting until the next night to catch Wallace Nussbaum. Mr. Galt is up and about when Walter returns home after his all-night adventure with "Sigerson." The climactic scene takes place in the building where Mr. Galt works. He pretends to pick the lock, but is actually using his key. Once inside, he quite literally stage manages things, placing Walter, Winston, and Rat in the wings of the darkened theater away from the adult hoaxers, then ordering the youths to catch Nussbaum in the aisles while he and the Mighty Gorilla "subdue" the nonexistent orangutan in the projection booth.

We have established not only that Mr. Galt is playing Sigerson, but that the entire novel is carefully crafted so that every character, incident, and detail is consistent with the staging of an entertainment by several playful adults for the three teenagers, as well as for their own enjoyment. Why is this significant?

Most importantly, it proves that the novel is not without a plot. Perhaps the reviewers who found *Avocado* overripe would not have regarded the novel any more favorably had they been aware of the hoax subplot. However, so much of the adverse criticism of *Avocado* was based on its alleged lack of structure, that the critics would have needed to completely rewrite their reviews and find something different to criticize if they had known of the mystery. For one thing, they had the genre wrong: *Avocado* is a comic mystery, not "a strange science fiction book."[22] There are no science fiction places, characters, or occurrences in the novel.

Perhaps the critics would reply that the mystery subplot is too subtle, and that if most readers don't detect it, it fails to help the novel. That is a legitimate point, and as we noted earlier, Pinkwater himself seemed surprised that so few had commented on the subplot. Perhaps he *was* too subtle. All the same, once the subplot has been revealed, one can no longer say that Pinkwater was a careless writer who dashed off an irrational, disconnected bit of slapstick. The slapstick in *Avocado* was provided not directly by the author, but by characters having fun playing double roles. Realization of that fact greatly increases enjoyment of the novel.

Early in *Avocado*, Pinkwater gives us a clue as to his idea of good comedy. Walter and Winston enjoy a Laurel and Hardy festival at the Snark so much that they leave the theatre "staggering around, weak from all that laughing." Walter explains what he likes about Laurel and Hardy films:

> Things happen at exactly the moment they have to happen. . . .You can even predict what's going to happen—and it does happen—and it surprises you anyway. It doesn't surprise you because it happened, but because it happened so perfectly. I laughed so hard that I cried. (15)

The end product of a Laurel and Hardy, Charlie Chaplin, or Marx Brothers film may be "silly" or "zany" slapstick, but perfectly executed slapstick is a high art. In its own way, *The Snarkout Boys and the Avocado of Death* is that kind of an achievement. Peter Andrews perceptively recognized that Pinkwater's deft handling of a "goofball" concept made *Slaves of Spiegel* a nearly perfect novella. However, Andrews and his fellow reviewers missed the mark when they failed to discern that *Avocado*, published by the same author in the same year, also has a logical underpinning.

The Snarkout Boys and the Avocado of Death is one of Pinkwater's richest novels. In most of his books Pinkwater throws off innumerable gag names and references, each of which he knows will be caught by only a few readers. *Avocado* is no exception, with a criminal orangutan (a send-up of Edgar Allan Poe's *Murders in the Rue Morgue*), and characters named Gutzman, Sigerson, and Sacker, the first taken from a famous film and both of the latter from Sherlock Holmes lore. Pinkwater's intellect should not be underestimated because he writes humorous books for children. So did Lewis Carroll, whose *Alice* books also have a superficial appearance of silliness and disorder.

The novel abounds with wonderful place names: Genghis Khan High School, Hun State University, and The Deadly Nightshade Diner—We Never Close, to name a few. There are colorful characters, such as Miss Sweet, the crazy biology teacher, and Captain Shep Nesterman, the intellectual street musician, with Dharmawati, his performing chicken. It is full of laugh-out-loud scenes, and offers some deliciously nostalgic, atmospheric settings: the nighttime bus rides to the Snark, the all-night movies and diners, Beanbender's wonderful beer garden, and walking tours of some great old neighborhoods.

One of the most attractive aspects of *Avocado* is the inclusion of interesting female characters, not ordinarily one of Pinkwater's strengths. Rat, a.k.a. Bentley Harrison Saunders Matthews, is a terrific character: tough, self-confident, and more than a match for the boys. She is totally convincing, and certainly one of Pinkwater's finest creations. Rat's mother, Minna Terwilliger Matthews, and Walter's mother, Mildred Galt, are delightful eccentrics, and both are given added depth when one views them as participants in the mystery hoax. The female cast of *Avocado* is an enormous improvement over that of *Alan Mendelsohn*, in which Leonard Neeble's clueless mother and a few miserable junior high school teachers are the only women in the novel. The excellent female personalities in *Avocado* complement Pinkwater's usual strong roster of male figures. Fortunately for us, many of the same characters re-appear in *The Snarkout Boys and the Baconburg Horror*.

NOTES

1. WH: "Is there any chance of another Snarkout book in the near future?" DP: "Doubtful." WH: "Can I complain to any publisher that they are depriving me of my basic rights to the entire Pinkwater oeuvre?" DP: "No. Never complain to publishers. They will just go home and yell at their kids." Email exchange between W. Hogan and D. Pinkwater, 30 November 1999.
2. Unsworth, Robert. *School Library Journal* (March 1982): 150.
3. *Kirkus Reviews* (1 March 1982): 276.
4. Peter Andrews, *New York Times* (25 April 1982): 51. The same issue also contained a separate review of Pinkwater's picture book, *Roger's Umbrella*, 38.
5. E. R. Twichell, *Horn Book* (July 1982): 292.
6. *Booklist* (15 March 1982): 961.
7. *Children's Book Review Service* (April 1982): 90.
8. Joann Davis, "Spring is a Season of Plenty for Children's Author Daniel Pinkwater ," *Publisher's Weekly* (7 May 1982): 53.
9. *Voice of Youth Advocates* (August 1982): 35.
10. *Kliatt Young Adult Paperback Guide* (spring 1983): 16.

11. Sigerson and Sacker look and behave exactly like Sherlock Holmes and Dr. Watson. In an online response to a fan question, Pinkwater explained the source of the characters' names: "just before publication Sir Arthur Conan Doyle was still calling his characters Sherrinford Holmes, and Dr. Ormond Sacker. And Sigerson was an alias Holmes used during his travels when thought to be dead, after Reichenbach Falls." *Talk to DP, Archive*, 14 (30 January 1999). Pinkwater also wrote a wonderful parody of Sherlock Holmes' experiences in India when the famous detective employed the alias of Sigerson, "Journal of a Ghurka Physician" in *The Game Is Afoot*, ed. Marvin Kaye (New York: St. Martin's, 1993).

12. Daniel Pinkwater, *The Snarkout Boys and the Avocado of Death* (New York: Morrow, 1982).

13. Twichell, 292.

14. Unsworth, 150.

15. *Kirkus*, 276.

16. Andrews, 51

17. Andrews, 51

18. Andrews, 51

19. *Talk to DP Forum, Archive*, 14 (30 January 1999).

20. Other such intellectually playful mystery novels come to mind: Umberto Eco's *Foucault's Pendulum* and *Name of the Rose*, the latter containing an homage to Sherlock Holmes in Brother William of Baskerville. Also Herman Hesse's *Steppenwolf*, with its play-within-the-novel, and some of the short stories of Jorge Luis Borges.

21. There are several enjoyable possibilities for the identities of Gutzman and the night watchman. They could have been played by Rat's father, Mr. Matthews; or by Uncle Flipping, who has "disappeared;" or perhaps by the Roosman brothers, owners of the warehouse where the night watchman was found (113). Roosman and Rassman, the delightfully eccentric pilots of *The Worms of Kukumlima*, would have been excellent recruits for Sigerson's hoax.

22. *Children's Book Review Service*, 90.

Chapter 7

The Snarkout Boys and the Baconburg Horror

In 1984, two years after publication of *The Snarkout Boys and the Avocado of Death*, Pinkwater brought out a sequel, *The Snarkout Boys and the Baconburg Horror*. Most of the characters are back, including the narrator of *Avocado*, Walter Galt, along with his friends Winston Bongo and Bentley Saunders Harrison Matthews, a.k.a. Rat. One of the first differences that strike readers of Pinkwater's two previous young adult novels, *Alan Mendelsohn* and *Avocado*, is the change in narrative perspective. Both of the earlier books employ straightforward first-person narration. However, *Baconburg* features multiple first person narrators, some third-person narration, as well as chapters entirely composed of "exhibits" such as newspaper clippings, memoranda, transcripts of local TV news broadcasts, and poems.

In fact, *Baconburg* opens with a spooky soliloquy by an apparent werewolf: "The moon rises. The leaves tremble in the night wind. Dark covers the city. I wait in my place of hiding."[1] The next chapter (each short chapter begins with an image of a werewolf's hairy hand/paw in place of a number) is narrated by the familiar voice of Walter Galt: "For more than a year, my friend Winston Bongo and I have been snarking out together" (9).

The critical reception of *Baconburg* was extremely positive. The novel was variously described as "refreshing,"[2] "a riotous treat,"[3] "hilarious,"[4,5] and "a very funny mystery."[6] Among the dozen contemporary reviews, only one was unfavorable. That review, by Heide Piehler, a librarian writing for *School Library Journal*, made several thoughtful comparisons between *Baconburg* and its predecessor, *Avocado*:

> The new characters are not as colorful as those in the earlier adventure and even the reappearing figures have less vitality than they did in the earlier book. . . . In the sequel, Walter's first-person narration is just one of several narrative styles. Without a stabilizing force, the humor isn't as polished or witty. There are a few genuine moments, but all in all, this book disappoints.[7]

Although her conclusions were at odds with most other reviews of *Baconburg*, Piehler's analysis of the relative merits of the two Snarkout books was well reasoned, and her stated reasons for preferring *Avocado* are sensible. Two other reviews, otherwise entirely favorable, agreed with Piehler's assertion that *Baconburg* was not the equal of its predecessor: "Pinkwater strikes again with a sequel to his superb *The Snarkout Boys and the Avocado of Death*. This isn't quite as good, but neither is 99% of all the fiction published this year."[8] Another noted, "It is a terrific book, nearly as good as the first, magical Snarkout Boys adventure."[9]

Although many of the reviews noted that *Baconburg* was a sequel, none of the other critics ventured a qualitative comparison of the two Snarkout novels. Most of the reviews of *Baconburg* were descriptive rather than analytical. Typically, the reviewer would begin by throwing around some of Pinkwater's funny names for persons and locations, then would describe *Baconburg* as some sort of wild and crazy romp, and finally wrap up with a favorable recommendation. The following is representative:

> Oh, Snorkle, gurgle, burpis and whee! Mix werewolves, borgelnuskies, the Nussbaum brothers and the Snarkout Boys. Put in locations such as the Deadly Nightshade Diner—We Never Close and the Garden of Earthly Bliss Drive-in and Pizzeria, and you've got another sure-fire Pinkwater hit. Crazy, erratic, silly and completely sophomoric here's the latest winner from one of the star authors in the junior high stable.[10]

Why did *Baconburg* receive better notices than its predecessor? Well, these were different reviewers, albeit writing for the same periodicals. As we have seen, some of the *Baconburg* reviewers claimed to have a high retrospective opinion of *Avocado*. However, the specific comments made by the reviewers of each novel make it clear that both Snarkout novels were universally regarded as zany romps. Nobody accused either novel of harboring any plot, structure, or deeper meaning. For some reason, the characteristic "zaniness" for which Pinkwater was criticized in 1982 had become a virtue by 1984. Essentially, reviewers of the first Snarkout novel agreed, "this book is too silly," while the reviewers of the sequel said, "this is a wonderfully wacky adventure, even better than its marvelous predecessor!"

It would appear that the author's overall reputation had grown during this period of phenomenal productivity; nobody had been calling him "one of the star authors in the junior high stable" back in 1982. A general rise in Pinkwater's stature is the most likely explanation for the sequel's better reception. Few readers of both Snarkout adventures will judge *Baconburg* to be a major improvement upon *Avocado*. Whatever its merits, the sequel is certainly not superior with respect to the specifics for which the earlier novel had been criticized: alleged silliness and looseness of plot, as we shall see.

Following the opening werewolf soliloquy, Walter Galt reacquaints us with his world. New readers are smoothly introduced to the characters and setting, without interruption of the narrative flow. After meeting Walter and Winston one night at the Snark, Rat leads them to the Dharma Buns Coffee House,[11] a beatnik cafe she has been wanting to visit. Rat is quite taken with the poet Jonathan Quicksilver, who chats with the three youths following his reading performance. Suddenly everyone leaves when the waitress is frightened by a supposed werewolf. Rat is followed home by the unseen werewolf-narrator.

On the following Saturday, Walter, Winston, and Rat visit the Grand Mall in the suburb of Hamfat. There they meet Jonathan Quicksilver's Guru, Lama Lumpo Smythe-Finkel, at Howling Frog's bookstore. Everyone has been talking about the werewolf, which the local media have begun calling "The Baconburg Horror." After being frightened by an invisible presence, Rat easily locates werewolf expert K. E. Kelman, PH (phantomologist), whom the FBI had been unable to find. Kelman's mother, Lydia LaZonga, exorcises Rat's soundproof room. Meanwhile, the Lama receives a paranormal warning about the werewolf.

Most of the book's characters converge at the Deadly Nightshade Diner—We Never Close. The archcriminal Wallace Nussbaum—allegedly the twin brother of Rat's butler Heinz—appears briefly to taunt Osgood Sigerson and threaten further mayhem by his "hypno-simulated werewolf." Sigerson instructs everyone to return on Thursday to gorge on borgelnuskies and then go werewolf-hunting.

The climactic scene occurs that Thursday night at the Garden of Earthly Bliss Drive-in and Pizzeria. Sigerson sends a dozen or so characters there with instructions to catch the werewolf during a werewolf movie festival. In a chaotic scene, Heinrich Nussbaum and his werewolf cavort, the werewolf pursuers run about with bouquets of wolfbane, and a local pyromaniac sets fire to the giant screen, setting off sprinklers which douse everyone and cause an automated pizza robot to run amok.

In a brief coda we hear that under the influence of plants administered by Wallace Nussbaum, Uncle Flipping had been transformed into the werewolf. Flipping is said to be recovering, and Wallace Nussbaum has been imprisoned in the Chateau d'If. But on the final page the sinister voice of Nussbaum breaks into the soundtrack of a movie at the Snark, and announces the villain's escape from that famous prison.[12]

What of the mystery subplot we traced in *Avocado*? Does *Baconburg* contain an equally rigorous substructure? Is the werewolf a hoax, as were the criminal orangutan and the Alligatron (the "Avocado of Death") of *Avocado*?

Due to its mix of narrative viewpoints, *Baconburg* cannot be quite the same sort of mystery as *Avocado*. That earlier book was narrated entirely by Walter Galt, who seemed to be taken in by his father's hoax. Seeing and hearing only through Walter's eyes and ears, the reader could achieve fuller understanding of the novel's events than offered by the narrator only by making more of the clues available to Walter than did Walter himself. However, in *Baconburg*, we are confronted with at least two narrators who provide us additional points of view that were absent from *Avocado*. These are the werewolf's first-person narration, and an omniscient narrator who describes events not seen by Walter.

Baconburg includes nine passages in which we are allowed insight into the werewolf's thoughts. Several of the werewolf's communiqués consist of only a couple of sentences. His longest narration is his first, slightly more than a page, which begins the book. In that opening passage the werewolf describes his physical transformation, "My nose gets longer. My skin tingles as fur sprouts everywhere. . . . My teeth are fangs now. My nails have turned hard and horny, and black and sharp" (7). On the next page he tells us, "Now I am ready to scamper down the exterior of the tall building" (8). Either this apparent werewolf's narration is unreliable, or else we are being asked to accept the existence of an unnatural, mythological being.

Vague near-sightings of the werewolf also appear to indicate the presence of a fantastic, abnormal creature. On several occasions, various people sense a presence which can't quite be seen. "A thick place in the air . . . a shadow where there shouldn't have been a shadow," is Rat's impression of an intruder who has inexplicably penetrated her locked, soundproof basement room (59).

Several passages of *Baconburg* are related by an omniscient narrator. Some of these sections present paranormal phenomena. In one such passage, we are allowed a glimpse into the home ("suburban yurt") of Lama Lumpo Smythe-Finkel. The lama is said to be "hovering an inch above the carpet." Then a book appears from nowhere, falls from the ceiling and into his hands. After he reads a page, "The book dematerializes. It is suddenly thin air. It is no more" (80-81).

These and numerous other episodes in *Baconburg* appear to assert the existence of a fantastic creature, as well as the occurrence of various supernatural events. Since Pinkwater is generally regarded as an author of science fiction and fantasy literature, in one sense this is all to be expected. The fantasy is only surprising in view of our awareness that all of the alleged paranormal events in *Baconburg*'s predecessor, *Avocado*, were cleverly faked by a group of actors. What happened to those actors in *Baconburg*?

Most of them have returned: Walter's parents, Theobald and Mildred Gault. Winston's Uncle, the Mighty Gorilla. Rat's Uncle, Flipping Hades Terwilliger, and her butler, Heinz. Those five were the main hoaxers in *Avocado*, and, with the help of a few bit players, they staged a very enjoyable farce. And it is quite possible that all of them are playing similar roles in *Baconburg*, along with some new characters such as K. E. Kelman and his mother. But unless some way is found to discount the werewolf narrator's claims and his physical near-invisibility, as well as several passages presented by an omniscient narrator, we are unable to conclude that the sequel, like its predecessor *Avocado*, was an entirely plausible hoax, staged to appear fantastic.

Moreover, an enormous amount of property destruction occurs in *Baconburg*: The werewolf begins by ripping off car doors and works up to the destruction of an entire drive-in theatre, with some help from a local pyromaniac, Ignatz the Igniter. This sort of public mayhem is in marked contrast with *Avocado*, which was carefully staged in safe, out-of-the-way locations such as an old warehouse and the disused theatre in Mr. Galt's office building. Nothing that occurred in *Avocado* would have drawn the attention of the media, police, and FBI, as do the werewolf's rampages in *Baconburg*.

At the end of *Baconburg*, Flipping Hades Terwilliger is identified as the werewolf. However, Uncle Flipping was one of the hoaxers in *Avocado*, and he might be hoaxing again in the sequel. Furthermore, the werewolf is infatuated with Rat and stalks her on several occasions. It would not be Pinkwater's style to suggest an incestuous connection between Uncle Flipping and his young niece. Therefore, the real werewolf, if there is one, might be another character in the story.

Suspicion falls upon the "avant-garde" poet, Jonathan Quicksilver, for a number of reasons: his Transylvanian origins, his knowledge of werewolves, and his enrollment in an evening civics class. The werewolf tells us, "I tear my civics textbook in two" (7). Like the werewolf, Quicksilver is a bad poet, although they are different sorts of bad poets: Quicksilver's poetry is trivial, maudlin, and prosaic. The werewolf's poems are silly, punning takeoffs on famous classical poetry. In addition, we have in the name "Jonathan Quicksilver" a possible combination of Jonathan Harker, a victim of Count Dracula,[13] with the changeable, "mercurial" element, mercury, or quicksilver.

However, the evidence is contradictory. The first time we meet Quicksilver, he is sitting at a table in the Dharma Buns Coffee House with Walter, Rat, and Winston when a werewolf apparently runs through the kitchen and is "sort of seen" by both Walter and the waitress. Later, Quicksilver is seated in the Deadly Nightshade Diner—We Never Close, again with numerous witnesses, while the werewolf narrator claims to be lurking in the bushes outside the diner. Quicksilver may be a werewolf, but if so, he cannot be the only werewolf in the story. Similarly, the hoaxers might be putting on another "entertainment," but if so, numerous paranormal events are left unexplained. Stumped, this author finally asked Daniel Pinkwater what was going on in *Baconburg*. Was Mr. Galt still playing Sigerson? Was the civics textbook a false lead—a red herring? His response:

> Nobody at all picked up on the Galt/Sigerson theme of *Avocado*, so I didn't feel there was much call to go to similar lengths in *Baconburg*—besides, it's a different book about different things. There aren't enough red herrings served up these days, don't you agree?[14]

We may not concur with Daniel Pinkwater that novels are improved by the insertion of misleading clues. But our struggles with *Baconburg* have at least provided us a proverb: Man who fishes in pink water may catch red herrings.

Other aspects of the novel may offer rosier prospects. What of public school education, a theme that was dominant in *Alan Mendelsohn*? The first Snarkout novel begins very much like the opening lines of that earlier novel, opening with Walter's complaint: "I thought going to high school was going to be a big improvement over what I was used to. It turned out to be just the opposite."[15]

Despite that similar beginning, the school experience turns out to be much less important in the Snarkout novels than it was in *Alan Mendelsohn*. The same ingredients are present, but Pinkwater uses them more sparingly, choosing instead to focus on evening and weekend extracurricular events. The early chapters of *Avocado* include some wonderful satire of life at Genghis Khan High School, especially the descriptions of the "notebook system" used for grading, and the senile biology teacher, Miss Sweet. There is not much reference to high school life in the sequel.

Walter and Winston are both short and squatty—in the mold of Leonard Neeble—and obviously not members of the "in crowd," but none of that seems to cause them much distress. Winston is described as an excellent wrestler, but we don't hear that he has any interest in the varsity wrestling team. Like their unconventional, green-haired friend Rat, who describes her classmates at George Armstrong Custer High School as "insects" and "subnerds,"[16] the boys seem comfortable being nonconformist outsiders at school.

In contrast with Leonard Neeble in *Alan Mendelsohn*, none of the three Snarkout youths are reported to be having any social or academic difficulties in the classroom. Essentially, Walter, Winston, and Rat come to us having already attained the state of mind that Leonard had painfully acquired by the end of *Alan Mendelsohn*, after months of misery. That is, they are dissatisfied with their respective schools, and they wish that their teachers, curricula, and classmates were more stimulating. However, they've found effective ways of coping. Walter, Winston, and Rat all have rich lives outside of school, featuring music appreciation, regular film viewing at the Snark, exploration of urban neighborhoods, auto mechanics and poetry for Rat, and wrestling for the boys.

As in most of Pinkwater's books, food is an important and pervasive theme. Walter describes his mother's lack of culinary talent: "My father believes in my mother's cooking. He says it will prepare me for life. He says his mother cooked just like my mother, and that nothing in this world frightens him" (27).

This echoes a passage from *Avocado*, in which Walter speaks of a discovery he shared with Winston: "Both of us had been victims of bad cooking since we were babies. Gradually, we realized that the food at home was horrible. We got clues from things like being the only kids at school who liked the school-cafeteria food better than what we got at home."[17]

Pinkwater also describes homes in which the cooking is eccentric, or nonexistent. Alan Mendelsohn's grandparents "eat basically what Lucky (their parrot) eats"(9). His grandmother "believes everything should be eaten raw—so there's no actual cooking" (175). Neither does the term "cooking" apply to the meals at Rat's home. Breakfast there consists of Chinese gooseberries, crunchy granola, and cornmeal muffins, all washed down with root beer.

In both Snarkout novels, the boys are excited to discover delicious cuisine in restaurants. The best and healthiest meal they sample is that served to them at Bignose's Cafeteria before the climactic scene of *Avocado*, a lovingly-described feast featuring salad with dandelion greens, baked lamb, and freshly-baked whole wheat bread. They also enjoy participating in the Thursday night borgelnuskies orgy at the

Deadly Nightshade Diner—We Never Close, although that indulgence is considerably less healthful. Walter describes the sight of the Mighty Gorilla eating nine one-foot-long borgelnuskies as a "frightening spectacle" (140). The characters also encounter some truly awful food establishments, such as the Dharma Buns Coffee House, offering only horrible coffee and "disgusting" cinnamon rolls, and Ms. Doughnut: "They make them fresh but they taste stale" (19). Pinkwater offers us the whole gamut of dining-out experiences. His characters persistently use diners and restaurants as meeting and gathering places, and these establishments—whether good or bad—usually have funny names and are always humorously and affectionately described.

In Pinkwater's novels, food is more than an incidental diversion; it is usually essential to the plot. The very title of the first Snarkout novel, and the constant references to avocados throughout both Snarkout books, are perhaps the most obvious examples. The werewolf in *Baconburg* is alleged to have been created "by feeding someone a decoction of the plant marifesa" (124). Pineapples and banana peels are said to be evidence left by a criminal orangutan. The deliriously chaotic finale of *Baconburg* is greatly enhanced by the malfunctioning of the robot pizza chef, as described in a verse of Wallace Nussbaum's psalm: "The Mitsubishi Medium-Range Pizza Chef spits hot cheese at mine enemies" (168).

Pinkwater does not hesitate to affirm the importance of food. He knows food of all kinds, and he describes it well. He explains the value of vegetarian and health foods, but also praises meat dishes. He discusses good cuisine, but also conveys the earthy gustatory pleasure of devouring greasy, salty snacks and rich desserts. He loves old-fashioned one-of-a-kind diners, but he also has fun describing modern fast food establishments.[18] Even when food is bad, as at the Hasty Tasty, Ms. Doughnut, and the Dharma Buns Coffee House, or as cooked by the mothers of most of his young protagonists, Pinkwater manages to salvage some entertainment value from such execrable fare by making fun of it. He always contrives to obtain pleasure from food and from the dining experience in one way or another.[19]

In addition to his special fondness for diners, Pinkwater populates his books with a wide range of mid-century cultural references. All of Pinkwater's young adult novels are saturated with nostalgia for the 1950s, the era of the author's own youth. Both of the Snarkout novels, of course, take their titles from the Snark Theater, a great old-fashioned movie theatre which runs classic movies late into the night.[20] *Avocado* is filled with wonderfully atmospheric scenes of Walter and his friends exploring lively, funky old neighborhoods at night. They hear speeches in Blueberry Park, discover Tintown and Beanbender's; and at Bignose's Cafeteria, they experience food so wonderful that Walter tells us, "it changed my life, and Winston's" (*Avocado*, 129).

Baconburg continues this rich nostalgic vein. Again, there are spooky nighttime walks and delicious meals at establishments like the Deadly Nightshade Diner—We Never Close. There is the fun of touring in Winston's 1958 Peugeot Super Grand Luxe Extra, and the pleasure of finding a distinctive establishment like Howling Frog—Books of the Weird in the otherwise sterile Grand Mall of Hamfat.

The most wonderful discovery of all is the Garden of Earthly Bliss Drive-in and Pizzeria, a gloriously tacky monument to the automobile culture and kitsch decorative styles of the 1950s. In addition to creating a fictional drive-in to end all drive-ins, Pinkwater entertains and informs with amusing newspaper clippings about the history of drive-in movie theaters.

Much of the uniqueness of Pinkwater's fictional world is derived from his particular combination of science fiction/fantasy elements with a special feeling for the 1950s. There is a sense in which these two elements merge and overlap in his fiction. They work together in complementary ways. The fantasy creates wonder and captures the imagination. Simultaneously, the grounding of the story in vividly described settings—often composites of places which strongly impressed the author during his youth in several large American cities—pulls one fully into the fictional setting and assists in enabling the reader's suspension of disbelief.[21]

Authors of imaginative fiction have long found the contrast of old-fashioned atmospheres with speculative ideas to be highly effective. The numerous reprintings and film remakes of Gothic and Victorian classics by Mary Shelley, Bram Stoker, Jules Verne, H. G. Wells, Robert Louis Stevenson, Lewis Carroll, and L. Frank Baum attest to the popularity of fantasies which combine futuristic elements with quaint, often nostalgic settings. A century later, we enjoy these settings even more—the sumptuous Victorian interior of the Nautilus, the superstitious Romanian villagers, the homely Kansas wheat farm. Whether Pinkwater will join those immortals is not yet known. But his storytelling technique of combining fantasy with vividly recollected memories of his youth is a classic one. That technique enlivens all of his novels, none more so than his wonderful Snarkout adventures, in both of which a fine balance between fantasy and genuine young adult experience is maintained.

NOTES

1. Daniel Pinkwater, *The Snarkout Boys and the Baconburg Horror* (New York: NAL Signet, 1984); hereafter cited in text as *Baconburg*.
2. *Horn Book* (Sept/Oct 1984): 594.
3. *Booklist* (1 September 1984): 70.
4. *Kirkus Reviews* (1 May 1984): J-49.
5. *Changing Times* (December 1984): 71.
6. Betsy Churchill, *Voice of Youth Advocates* (October 1985): 284.
7. Heide Piehler, *School Library Journal* (May 1984): 92.
8. *Science Fiction Chronicle* (October 1985): 44.
9. Michael Dirda, "The Chicken at the Edge of the Universe," *Washington Post Book World* (10 June 1984): 6.
10. Susan B. Madden, *Voice of Youth Advocates* (August 1984): 144.
11. Derived from *The Dharma Bums* by Jack Kerouac.
12. The Chateau d'If is a fictional island prison from Alexandre Dumas' *The Count of Monte Cristo* (1846).
13. Pinkwater named characters after Jonathan Harker and Professor Van Helsing—both from Bram Stoker's *Dracula* (1897)—in his picture book, *I Was a Second Grade Werewolf* (1983). Thus, it is not far-fetched to suggest that in another of Pinkwater's werewolf stories, a Transylvanian named Jonathan might be more than he seems.
14. Email from D. Pinkwater to W. Hogan, 14 February 2000.
15. Daniel Pinkwater, *The Snarkout Boys and the Avocado of Death* (New York: Morrow, 1982), 1.
16. *Avocado*, 40.
17. *Avocado*, 120.
18. Pinkwater's picture book, *Spaceburger*, displays some of the author's tastes. Spaceburger is a new fast food outlet, much like any other hamburger franchise, but the boys like it a lot better because it has a 1950s-1960s-style spaceship theme. Daniel Pinkwater, *Spaceburger, a Mason Mintz and Kevin Spoon Story* (New York: Macmillan, 1993).
19. Pinkwater's descriptions of bad home cooking in several of his books apparently have a real-life basis. He comments that "My mother was a lousy cook," and continues, "Where I live nowadays, in the country, you occasionally run into tree-dwellers who believe there's an international Jewish conspiracy. There is one. It's the utter fiction Jews put forth that their mothers could cook." Daniel Pinkwater, *Hoboken Fish and Chicago Whistle* (Princeton, N.J.: Xlibris, 1999), 100.
20. The Snark is modeled after the Clark Theater in Chicago. *The (Sort of) Official Daniel Pinkwater Website, Talk to DP Forum, Archive*, 7 <*http://www.designfoundry.com/p-zone*> (16 September 1998); also *Hoboken Fish*, 66-68.
21. Pinkwater has said that his "mental urban model was an amalgamation of Chicago and Los Angeles, with specific excerpts from New York, London, and Cincinnati, a shot of the White Castle in Cleveland at 2:00 a.m., and a certain

intersection in the old part of Nairobi." *Talk to DP Forum, Archive*, 9 (16 September 1998).

Chapter 8

Young Adult Novel

In 1982, the same year during which Pinkwater brought out *The Snark-out Boys and the Avocado of Death*, he also published a picture book (*Roger's Umbrella*) and two remarkable short novels, or novellas. *Slaves of Spiegel*, a seventy-three page book, was the final volume of the Magic Moscow trilogy featuring the adventures of narrator Norman Bleistift and his friend and employer, Steve Nickelson.[1] *Slaves*, targeted at the mid-grade audience, is revered by readers of all ages as Pinkwater's most delicious and perfect comedy. The other short novel published in that banner year was the fifty-eight page *Young Adult Novel*. This superb pair of novellas were reprinted together fifteen years later, as two of the five stories chosen for inclusion in the first Pinkwater omnibus, *5 Novels* (1997).

The opening chapter of *Young Adult Novel* is a shocker. We are told of a thirteen-year-old "alcoholic, pusher, and thief," Kevin Shapiro, whose mother is in a "madhouse," while his father has "been deprived of speech, sight, and hearing, and the use of his legs," and his sister is "turning tricks on State Street."[2] Although these tragic circumstances are described in a straightforward, sympathetic manner, they do seem a bit excessive, so readers unfamiliar with Pinkwater's satirical bent might be uncertain whether this story should be read as a sincere narrative. The chapter's conclusion decisively resolves any confusion on that score: "It seemed to Kevin that there wasn't a chance in the world that he would ever get his life straightened out. And he was right. So we hit him over the head and fed him to the pigs" (3).

It turns out that inventing such stories about the imaginary "Kevin Shapiro, Boy Orphan" is one of the hobbies of a group of five male high school students who call themselves the Wild Dada Ducks. There are three additional "Boy Orphan" stories in the novel, otherwise the remainder of the book is a first-person narration by one of the five Dada Ducks, Charles the Cat.[3] All of the Wild Dada Ducks have forsaken their given names for ones they have invented: the remaining four are known to us only as the Honorable Venustiano Carranza (President of Mexico),[4] Captain Colossal, Igor, and the Indiana Zephyr.

The next several chapters detail the activities of the Wild Dada Ducks, primarily at Himmler High School. The boys have only a foggy conception of the historical Dada Movement: Charles explains that he had supposed Marcel Duchamp and Dada to be inventions of his friend, the Honorable . . . until after "I had been a Dadaist myself for months" (7). Nevertheless, they contrive to carry out a number of culturally re-bellious projects that are very much in the spirit of the original Dada movement, which flourished in Europe at the end of the First World War. These latter-day Dada performances by the Ducks include the circulation of an absurd manifesto, the staging of a nonsensical play in the school lunchroom, and the installation of a spotlessly clean porce-lain toilet in the school's trophy cabinet.[5] Such activities do not endear the Wild Dada Ducks to their classmates, nor to the Himmler High teachers and administration. However, they stubbornly persist.

The story takes a new turn when the Ducks discover that there is, by chance, a real student named Kevin Shapiro in their school. They decide that their next Dada project will be to publicize this actual Kevin Shapiro, and to make the hitherto obscure Kevin famous among the four thousand students of Himmler High. Kevin is a dull, colorless, completely undistinguished youth, and moreover, he warns the Ducks that he wants to be left alone. But again, they persist.

Unbeknownst to the Ducks, a student council election is imminent. So it transpires that the very day on which they have undertaken to dis-tribute two thousand colorful Dadaist cards proclaiming the greatness of Kevin Shapiro happens to be election day for the seven positions on student council. His name having just been brought so dramatically to everyone's attention, Kevin wins all seven places, including president, as a write-in candidate. Although Kevin publicly declines the honor, and the school principal "abolishes school elections until further no-tice," (42) Kevin has become a popular hero. The Dada Ducks are pleased with their accomplishment, and are "all very proud of him" (43).

The final third of *YAN* describes the consequences of Kevin Sha-piro's sudden and unexpected elevation from obscurity. As he leaves the stage following his terse rejection of student council, Kevin tells the Ducks, "I'll get you for this" (46). While we await Kevin's revenge, other unusual developments unfold. "It was on the third day after the election that the Fanatical Praetorians first appeared" (48). These Praetorians are uniformly short boys who wear sailor hats and serve as Kevin Shapiro's personal bodyguard.[6] Despite their small stature and silly costume, the numerousness and discipline of the Fanatical Praeto-rians allows them—and through them their leader, Kevin Shapiro—to effectively control the school in defiance of teachers, administration, and all pre-existing student elites. Kevin's appearance and personality seem totally lacking in charm or charisma. "Nevertheless, Kevin Shapiro had become undisputed king of Himmler High. His word was law. Of course, he practically never said anything, but if he had said anything, it would have been law" (49-50).

Kevin's only interest is in reading, trading, and collecting comic books. This pursuit is slavishly imitated by Kevin's followers, and their immersion in comic books is elevated to the status of an art movement which they call Heroic Realism.

The other notable characteristic of Kevin's behavior is his remarkably bland luncheon routine. Kevin's invariable noon meal in the school cafeteria consists of an individual packet of Grape-Nuts cereal, over which he pours a carton of milk. One day, Kevin stands up in the cafeteria and makes his first public utterance since the election. "Grape-Nuts is good!" (54). From that day forward, under the supervision of the Fanatical Praetorians, everyone in the school, even the Dada Ducks, eats nothing else for lunch.

In the climactic scene, we find that Kevin had a special motive for wanting all of his schoolmates to join him in his monotonous luncheon ritual. Shouting "Down with Dada!" and throwing his soggy Grape-Nuts in the face of the Honorable Venustiana Carranza (President of Mexico), he instigates a food massacre of the Wild Dada Ducks by all 1,000 students in the cafeteria (56). This is the perfect revenge: the Ducks themselves have been transformed into a Dada sculpture.

Following this dramatic event, things return to normal. Kevin does not exploit his power any further, and chooses to return to the obscurity from whence he had arisen. The Dada Ducks "suspended our program of cultural improvement for our fellow students" (58). As they try to decide what lessons to draw from the affair, the Honorable Venustiana Carranza (President of Mexico) has the final words: "It has no moral. . . it is a Dada story" (58).

What is the meaning of *YAN*? Although Pinkwater might support the assertion of the Honorable Venustiana Carranza (President of Mexico) that there is none, we will consider three.

First, *YAN* is a satire of the "problem novels" written by adults for teenage readers. Ten different reviewers of *YAN* made this point, variously describing the book as, "a dandy spoof of the modern YA novel,"[7] "a parody of the banal young adult novel,"[8] a sendup "of most of the cliches of the contemporary teenage novel,"[9] and "an irreverent parody of motifs found in contemporary young adult problem fiction."[10] As Charles the Cat explains, "*Kevin Shapiro, Boy Orphan* is different from the novels in the Himmler High School Library in that he never resolves his problems" (4-5). In an article celebrating Pinkwater's four 1982 books, the author told an interviewer, "I did finally read a few of the so-called "problem novels," and I was disgusted. I thought they were sneaky books; they imposed an adult point of view and morality on kids under the pretext of telling a story."[11]

Many of the novels written for young readers at that time carried a "constructive" moral message. This was not necessarily because the author was a fervent believer in what he preached. More likely, the moral overtones were calculated to ingratiate the author and his books with "the establishment." That is, with those adult publishers, book reviewers, teachers, school boards, librarians, and parents, who individually and collectively exert enormous control over minors' access to literature. Moreover, by the early 1980s these problem novels had apparently become something of a fad. In a 1982 essay, Patty Campbell noted that because YA fiction was easier to get published than adult fiction, "the word is out—YA fiction is the way to go," resulting in a deluge of mediocre adolescent fiction. Campbell concurred with most reviewers of *Young Adult Novel* that Pinkwater's satire of the genre was timely and well-aimed, calling the book "an absolutely exquisite put-down, a piece of delicious dada fluff."[12]

The second layer of meaning that might be traced in *YAN* was put forth in a periodical that does not usually concern itself with juvenile literature. Greil Marcus, a former *Rolling Stone* editor, and the author of highly-regarded books and articles on popular culture, was for many years a contributing editor of the slick, avant-garde periodical, *Artforum International*. His regular column, "Greil Marcus' Top Ten," now published in the online journal *Salon.com*, reviews noteworthy artistic contributions in all media. Marcus once chose *Young Adult Novel* as one of his Top Ten:

> This really is a "young adult novel"—in which five high school washouts reform as the Wild Dada Ducks, levy fines on each other for such crimes as uttering the word "life-style," and foment a prank that leads to the election of the school's least-known student to all student offices, his transformation into a dictator with absolute power, and the defeat of Dada by Heroic Realism. In other words, a parable of the 1918 Berlin Dada club as a crucible for Nazism.[13]

Is this review overwrought? Can Pinkwater's little fifty-eight-page farce really bear such intellectual weight as Marcus suggests? We have noted that Pinkwater was a sculptor and printmaker before he became a writer, so we should not be surprised that he might draw from the history of art in his novels. A brief review of Dada will be necessary. The Dada Movement began in reaction to the horrors of the First World War. During that terrible war, while young men died in muddy trenches by the hundreds of thousands, artists began to realize that traditional art forms were incapable of making any meaningful statement about the contemporary world. Moreover, the entire business of art and culture, as exemplified by galleries and museums, and the publishing and theatrical entertainment industries, was controlled by vested interests and was inherently reactionary. Dada artists and writers wanted to disturb status-quo complacency and conformity. Many Dada works were disposable; their function was not to endure as beautiful objects, but rather to shock each viewer momentarily out of her normal secure and complacent worldview. Hence urinals displayed as art works, bicycle wheels mounted on wooden stools, flatirons with iron spikes, and the like.[14]

In New York, Paris, and Zurich, most of the Dadaists were apolitical and had no designs beyond shaking up the art world and expanding the opportunities for fresh artistic expression. Many of those artists participated in several early twentieth-century art movements in turn— Cubism, Futurism, Surrealism, Expressionism—and Dada was simply the dominant style during one brief phase of their careers.

However, some of the Berlin Dadaists were absorbed with the chaotic political situation in their country, and for them Dada was inextricably linked with public activism. In that hothouse environment it would have been difficult to remain neutral; there were street riots in Germany at the end of the war, and enormous civil unrest from 1917 to 1919, before the abdication of the Kaiser, the breakup of the Empire and the formation of the Weimar Republic.

> There was a revolution going on, and Dada was right in the thick of
> it. At one moment they were all for the *Spartakus* movement; then it
> was Communism, Bolshevism, Anarchism and whatever else was
> going.[15]

These Dadaists were as discontented with the new Weimar Republic as they had been with the old German Empire. They found Dada to be an excellent tool for political agitation. The Dada artist George Grosz became a renowned political cartoonist. In 1920, the First International Dada Fair in Berlin featured numerous subversive works, including a suspended dummy of a uniformed German officer with the head of a pig.[16] By fomenting disrespect for their weak, bourgeois government and failed military establishment, the Dadaists unwittingly contributed to the eventual rise of a Fascist dictatorship. Hence Greil Marcus' description of the Berlin Dada Club "as a crucible for Nazism." Hitler's Third Reich indeed emerged from this unrest, some of which was stirred up by provocative, satirical artists and entertainers.[17] Hans Richter, who was there, put it thus:

> This anarchistic spirit enabled the Berlin Dada movement to live life to the full, in its own way. It provides some excuse for even the most revolting lapses of taste and for all the violent manifestoes that sometimes even have a Nazi ring to them.[18]

But how do we make the leap from pre-Nazi Berlin to 1982 American suburbia?[19] The name of the boys' school, Himmler High, is an obvious link. Although Pinkwater often gives his schools improbable names—Bat Masterton Junior High, Genghis Khan High, etc.—this sinister appellation is rather more significant.[20]

Let's review the events of *Young Adult Novel*, this time in a strictly political context. The Wild Dada Ducks, an outcast group of nonconformist, intellectual misfits, use art to protest against an unimaginative and ineffectual authority structure: the administration of Himmler High. Their counter-cultural projects do not earn recognition or popularity for the Ducks themselves. Rather the reverse. Nevertheless, their actions do eventually bring about real, albeit unintended political consequences. Administration is shown to be weak and inept. The unlikely and untalented Kevin Shapiro effectively becomes dictator of the school. Administration claims to have cancelled student council and the electoral process, but the impotence of their rule has been fatally exposed.

Having been elevated by popular acclaim, on the basis of his sneering contempt for tradition and authority, Shapiro does not need teachers or administrators to legitimatize his power. He is soon surrounded by Fanatical Praetorians, an unauthorized militia who effectively police student behavior in accordance with the wishes of their leader.

Under Kevin Shapiro's cultural banner, Heroic Realism, the worlds of art and literature are reduced and restricted to comic books. The only approved food is a single brand of breakfast cereal, soaked with milk. When school authorities attempt to suppress the Praetorians by outlawing their sailor hats, the Praetorians are abetted by the entire school population in a successful defiance. Ultimately, Kevin Shapiro and his Fanatical Praetorians publicly humiliate a despised minority, and again the entire school body joins in the persecution. The Ducks, who had brought Kevin to power, are made scapegoats. Finally, the regime comes to an end, and everyone soon forgets all about the brief but spectacular reign of Kevin Shapiro and his Fanatical Praetorians. Note the similarly to actual events in post-World War I Germany. Members of the Berlin Dada Club, a fringe group of dissident artists, begin using Dada's capacity for mockery to satirize the political establishment. The weak government has no effective response to its critics. Although the Dadaists themselves do not generally achieve wide popularity, they do fan the flames of contempt for the Weimar government. But when that government is finally replaced by the Nazis, the Dadaists are precisely the sort of persons who become persecuted: artists, intellectuals, nonconformists, socialists, and anarchists.

The Nazi leader is an uneducated wallpaper hanger and former army corporal, a funny little fellow with very narrow interests, and who eats the blandest possible food. Nevertheless, everyone is cowed by his jackbooted, brownshirted paramilitary thugs, who carry out book burnings and forbid any art or literature that does not glorify their regime and its values. All art must be realistic (satirical and avant-garde forms are condemned as "decadent"); and heroic, as in Wagner's music, Reifenstahl's films, and monumental Nazi public architecture. Minorities such as Jews, gypsies, intellectuals, the handicapped, and the unfit are publicly humiliated and persecuted. Nearly all of the "regular" population supports the regime. But when the Nazis are finally defeated, everyone is eager to forget about them and their crimes.

Pinkwater's little book contains a rather faithful adaptation of those historical events to a modern high school setting. But this is not to say that *YAN* is merely a systematic allegory. Pinkwater's story is broadly allusive and resonates with archetypal patterns of human social behavior. Although *YAN* is modeled most specifically upon interwar Germany, in broader terms it describes a cycle that has been repeated throughout history, for example in both the French and Russian revolutions. Leading critics of a traditional, conservative government are often martyred by the revolutionary forces which they inspired and helped to power. Thus were Robespierre and Trotsky[21] consumed by the revolutions they had sparked.

One lesson of this tale is the danger of mixing politics with art. Dada has a valued place in art history. It influenced many artists to break away from old paradigms and to open up new creative vistas. However, it was also used as a revolutionary weapon, and as such it was a double-edged sword, perilous to those who would wield it. When the Wild Dada Ducks began using their art to try to change the real world, rather than just producing art for its own sake, they unleashed forces antithetical to their own interests and values.

This leads to the second moral lesson: one's fellow citizens are a potential mob that can become more dangerous than the onerous but predictable existing power structure. As depicted in such classic tales as George Orwell's *Animal Farm* and William Golding's *Lord of the Flies*, anarchy may not be preferable to a despised old order.

Thus far we have considered *Young Adult Novel* as a satire of adolescent problem novels, and as a parable of the danger of mixing art with politics. The third and final approach to *YAN* that we should consider is that this short novel simply represents an alternative approach by the author to one of his favorite subjects, the American public school experience. Pinkwater told an interviewer: "I'm not a great fan of Dada . . . but it does seem to reflect the point of view of a high school freshman. I'm in constant correspondence with my readers, and there are real groups very similar to the Wild Dada Ducks."[22]

Dada is the ideal tool for Pinkwater's ironic objectives in this book. Just as Dada was an anti-art movement (the Dadaists resisted becoming an "–ism," as in Impressionism, Cubism, etc.) *YAN* is an anti-novel. Not only is it a satire of problem novels by other authors, but it is also a darker, possibly self-parodying treatment of the subject matter of Pinkwater's own previous novels. Following his negative appraisal of contemporary problem novels, Pinkwater described *YAN* as "a cheap, nasty little book, as much like the others as I could make it."[23] The book has none of the nostalgic atmosphere or light comedy which sweetens *Alan Mendelsohn* and the Snarkout novels.[24] There is no happy ending, and there are no positive characters in the entire book: no Alan Mendelsohn from Mars or Osgood Sigerson from 221B Baker Street to come to the rescue. Nor can we identify with the five protagonists, who are not much differentiated, and whose real names we are never told.

In contrast to his earlier novels, in which individualism is celebrated, *YAN* explores the dark side of nonconformist behavior. The Ducks are terribly self-centered and egotistical. They are seriously alienated from their social milieu, as demonstrated by their serene assurance that they had been completely discreet in spying on Kevin Shapiro. In fact, Shapiro was immediately aware of their clumsy inquiries. The Ducks consistently refuse to make small compromises that would allow them to fit in better. Instead, they go out of their way to draw adverse attention to themselves: the Honorable Venustiano Carranza (President of Mexico) wears the wheel from a baby carriage on a chain around his neck, and Igor "has a banana on a string which he wears around his neck. He talks with the banana, whose name is Freddie, and also uses it as a mock microphone and make-believe pistol" (8-9).

As in many of Pinkwater's novels, we are given an imaginative adolescent narrator, who along with his friends struggles against a bad school, dull teachers, and shallow, conformist fellow students. Normally such protagonists would be Pinkwater's heroes. But these Ducks don't have enough sense to come in from the rain! No wonder they end up dripping and soggy. Three years later, Pinkwater would bring out *Young Adults*, a sequel to *YAN*, and as we'll see, the Ducks didn't get much smarter during those three years.

NOTES

1. The others are *The Magic Moscow* (1980) and *Attila the Pun* (1981).
2. Daniel Pinkwater, *Young Adult Novel* (New York: Crowell, 1982), 1-3; hereafter cited in text as *YAN*.
3. The novel is dedicated "To Charles—more than a cat," an actual cat belonging to the author, after whom the novel's narrator is named.
4. The real Carranza (1859-1920) was president of Mexico from 1915 until his assassination in 1920.
5. This last project, including its rejection by the authorities, echoes almost exactly the famous attempt by "the dean of Dada," Marcel Duchamp, to enter a porcelain urinal entitled "The Fountain" into an art exhibition at a New York museum in 1917. The urinal was later beautifully photographed by Alfred Stieglitz, and a large black-and-white print from that photograph has often been displayed as an art work. (Marc Dachy, *The Dada Movement, 1915-1923* [New York: Rizzoli, 1990], 82-83.)
6. The *cohors praetoria* existed by the second century BC, acting as bodyguards for Roman generals. In 27 BC the emperor Augustus created a permanent corps (the Praetorian Guard) . . . which became household troops of the Roman emperors. (*Encyclopedia Britannica Online* <http://britannica.com> [2 November 1999]) The brigades formed to guard the persons of later tyrants such as Adolf Hitler and numerous Latin American military dictators have also been described as Praetorian guards.
7. Unsworth, Robert, *School Library Journal* (May 1982): 74.
8. *Kirkus Review* (1 March 1982): 278.
9. *Washington Post Book World* (1 December 1985): 11.
10. *Horn Book* (June 1982): 301.
11. *Publisher's Weekly* (7 May 1982): 53-54.
12. Patty Campbell, "The Young Adult Perplex," *Wilson Library Bulletin* (March 1982): 533.
13. Greil Marcus, "Top Ten," *Artforum International* (February 1992): 24-25.
14. Respectively, Marcel Duchamp's *Fountain* (1915), his *Bicycle Wheel* (1913), and Man Ray's *Gift* (1921).
15. Hans Richter, *Dada: Art and Anti-Art* (New York: McGraw-Hill, 1965), 109.
16. Dachy, *The Dada Movement, 1915-1923.*

17. The life of artists in Berlin during the period leading up to Hitler's ascendancy has been depicted in several excellent films, including *Cabaret* (1972) and *Mephisto* (1981).

18. Richter, 113.

19. Although the setting of *YAN* is not specified, we should probably think of it as being in the general vicinity of Hogboro and Baconburg. The *Hoboken Chicken Emergencyclopedia* <http://home.earthlink.net/~stoba/hoboken> (5 November 1999) suggests that the exact location might be West Kangaroo Park, the suburb of Hogboro to which Alan Mendelsohn's family moved after leaving "the old neighborhood."

20. The school is actually called Margaret Himmler High, but the frequent references simply to "Himmler High" are clearly intended to suggest Heinrich Himmler (1900-1945), one of Adolf Hitler's most notorious henchman. As chief of the SS, which included the Nazi secret police or Gestapo, Himmler oversaw Nazi death squads, deportations and concentration camps.

21. Robespierre, (1758-1794) an early leader of the French Revolution, was ultimately sent to the guillotine like thousands of his victims before him. Leon Trotsky, (1879-1940) an early leader of the Russian Revolution, was banished and later assassinated by his Marxist rivals.

22. *Publisher's Weekly* (7 May 1982): 54.

23. *Publisher's Weekly* (7 May 1982): 54.

24. Pinkwater's usual satirical mode is Horatian, but in *YAN* it approaches that of Juvenal: "The character of the satirist as projected by Horace is that of an urbane man of the world, concerned about folly, which he sees everywhere, but moved to laughter rather than rage. Juvenal, more than a century later, conceives the satirist's role differently. His most characteristic posture is that of the upright man who looks with horror on the corruptions of his time, his heart consumed with anger and frustration." "Satire," *Merriam-Webster's Encyclopedia of Literature*, 1995, *Literature Resource Center* (Farmington Hills, MI: Gale Group). Online, GaleNet <http://www.galenet.com> (15 June 2000).

Chapter 9

Young Adults

Following publication of *Young Adult Novel* in 1982, Pinkwater brought out a sequel, *Young Adults*, in 1985. That sequel, a 224-page TOR paperback, contained a reprinting of *Young Adult Novel*; two new short pieces, *Dead-End Dada* and *The Dada Boys in Collitch*; plus an afterword, *The Confessions of Pinkwater*, by Ken Kelman. *Young Adults* also featured several multi-page computer-produced cartoon sequences, *The Buttoniad*, *Pigamorphosis*, and *W. A. Mozart, Superhero* (Parts I and II).[1] An abbreviated paperback version of *Young Adults* (minus the cartoons and afterword) was later issued by the same publisher. The unique material from *Young Adults*—i.e., all but the reprinted *Young Adult Novel*—is out of print at the time of this book's preparation, alone among the author's fiction for young adults.

Young Adults departs from Pinkwater's previous publications in several respects. As previously noted, the book includes several short works of fiction, all but one of them new. Although some of Pinkwater's novels have been reprinted together, nearly all of his fictional works, however brief, have originally been issued as individual clothbound monographs.[2] Another unusual feature of *Young Adults* is that some of its text is attributed to writers other than Pinkwater himself. In addition to *The Confessions of Pinkwater*, by Ken Kelman, *Dead End Dada* begins with contributions Pinkwater says were submitted to him by readers of *Young Adult Novel*. By far the most significant departure is the book's explicit sexual content. The review in *Kliatt Young Adult Paperback Guide* concluded with the following statement: "(Note: unlike the author's previous novels, this book contains profanity and humorous references to masturbation and sexual intercourse.)"[3]

We noted earlier that *Alan Mendelsohn* in 1979 was a breakthrough novel in that it marked a transition for Pinkwater from being an author of books for children to an author who also wrote for and about adolescents. From 1979 through 1985, when *Young Adults* was published, Pinkwater produced several novels with teenage protagonists, including *Young Adult Novel* and both Snarkout novels.

Young Adults represented a breakthrough to yet another readership level. The protagonists are older: in the two new stories the Ducks finish high school and go on to college. These characters are closer to the adult end of adolescence, so quite naturally, their preoccupations are different than those of the pre-adolescent or early adolescent protagonists of Pinkwater's earlier novels.

In *Young Adults*, Pinkwater took full advantage of his first opportunity to demonstrate that he is just as funny when writing about sex as he is on any other topic. However, as evidenced by the warning note appended to the *Kliatt* review, an author of books for children who tackles sexual topics is also taking on some career risks. None of Pinkwater's young adult novels appear on the long list of challenged and banned titles maintained by the American Library Association's Office of Intellectual Freedom.[4] Nevertheless, when he brought out *Young Adults*, Pinkwater effectively joined authors like Judy Blume who have risked adverse publicity and possible loss of some book sales, by choosing to address elements of the adolescent experience that some would prefer to suppress.

Critical response to *Young Adults* necessarily included reactions to *Young Adult Novel*, since that short novel was reprinted with the new stories. Perhaps surprisingly, since the earlier book had received a few negative reviews (amidst many positive ones) upon its publication in 1982, there were no hostile responses to the sequel. Michael Dirda, who has consistently praised Pinkwater's books in *Washington Post Book World*, gave *Young Adults* a warm reception.[5] Jack Lechner's substantial essay on Pinkwater in the *Village Voice* included favorable mention of *Young Adults*.[6] The *Kliatt* review was generally positive, with some reservations:

> Pinkwater is often hilarious, but he can be self-indulgent and needlessly obscure as well. His references . . . and his parodies . . . will probably be much funnier to adults than to most teens. . . . Still, for those special readers who get the joke, Pinkwater is a riotous revelation.[7]

Most of the reviews treated *Young Adults* as a whole, without much individual attention to the several stories. We will want to examine each of the new pieces, in the order of their appearance in the book.

Dead-End Dada

Dead-End Dada contains six pages of preliminary material, followed by a thirty-page story in thirteen chapters. The story is dedicated "to the spirit of Lieutenant Hiroo Onada," who hid on a Philippine island for over three decades, "not knowing that World War II had ended."[8] Following *Young Adult Novel*, this dedication prepares us for yet another hopeless, quixotic adventure with the Dada Ducks. We can be confident that the boys will continue to pursue lost causes, tilting at windmills, and succeeding only in bringing further ridicule upon themselves.[9]

The dedication is followed by a special section introduced by the author. Pinkwater tells us that the (four) "Kevin Shapiro, Boy Orphan" stories imbedded in *Young Adult Novel* had inspired a number of readers to submit "additional chapters of the story-within-a-story" (79). Pinkwater offers us seven of these contributions, appending a brief comment to each. The preliminary section ends with a 200-word author statement in which Pinkwater offers us an ironic mock-apology for his "sinister" publications, and claims it is his "devout hope that in time he may be able to produce acceptable books about cute furry animals and—for the older reader—stories about high schools in California with really good athletic programs and uniformly attractive students." But in the meantime, he entreats "teachers and librarians of the better sort to keep the book out of the hands of the young" (83).

The story proper, like *Young Adult Novel*, is narrated by Charles the Cat. Charles begins with a monologue in which he ponders the "inevitability" of nuclear war, and explains that in view of the impending crisis, the Ducks felt the need to find a new philosophy. They decide to abandon Dada in favor of Zen, although they know even less about the latter than they had about their former guiding principle. Zen having gone out of fashion a few years earlier, they are only able to find one Zen-related book at the local library, a Zen cookbook.

The boys continue to meet at the spot where their former gathering place—the Balkan Falcon Drug Company—had once stood, even though the old soda fountain has been replaced by a laundromat. The boys call the place the "Balkan Falcon Memorial Laundromat and Shrine of Buddha" (96). While sitting in the laundromat/shrine attempting to intuit a comprehensive Zen philosophy from the cookbook, the boys decide that the proprietor of the laundromat, a rather ordinary Chinese fellow named Sigmund Yee,[10] is a Zen master. Comical misunderstandings between the Ducks and Master Yee ensue.

At roughly the midpoint of *Dead-End Dada*, Kevin Shapiro, the boys' nemesis from *Young Adult Novel*, makes a striking reappearance. Kevin is driving a classic red convertible and is accompanied by three beautiful and adoring cheerleaders. Barely noticing the Ducks (who now call themselves the Dharma Ducks) Kevin causes them further anguish at every turn by virtue of his conspicuous, seemingly undeserved successes.

Meanwhile, the principal of Himmler High has required the Ducks to be assessed by Dr. Cookie Mendoza, the Board of Education psychiatrist. In her waiting room, the boys overhear her telling another boy that masturbation is nothing to be ashamed of. Since Dr. Mendoza claims to approve the practice as therapeutic and beneficial, the boys decide it would be a clever and harmless diversion to tell her that masturbation is their recreational pastime of choice. She goes to great lengths to reassure them that this is perfectly healthy and normal. Then she reports them to the school principal and to their parents as "vicious little perverts . . . utterly preoccupied with unwholesome practices" (110).

The boys are severely disciplined by their parents, besides undergoing further ostracism at school. They are thrown out of the laundromat by their "Zen Master," Mr. Yee. Their misery is deepened by periodic sightings of Kevin Shapiro flaunting his red convertible and his beautiful cheerleaders. Kevin is rumored to have been accepted into Princeton. In the final chapter, the Ducks, who are failing most of their classes, ponder their miserable fate. "Zen sucks," and "life stinks" are two of their pronouncements (113). They commence one of their five-kazoo concerts, as the story ends.

Dead-End Dada is a worthy sequel to *Young Adult Novel*. Pinkwater wrote the earlier book as an immediate response to his disgust with the conventional sort of adolescent problem novels. As numerous reviewers of *YAN* agreed, his lampoon of that genre was dead-on. Moreover, the novel provided Pinkwater an opportunity to work out a clever modern fable, based upon the historical Dada movement. This opened up fresh approaches to one of the author's favorite themes: the struggle of the creative imagination against a prevailing atmosphere of shallowness, conformity, and repression; played out in a favorite setting, the American public school. Following that excellent novel, *DED* accomplishes exactly what is required of a good sequel: taking its characters and setting from a previous story, it mines even greater riches from that situation.

Dada is replaced by Zen. The boys' new attachment allows Pinkwater to do for Zen what *YAN* had done for Dada. As in his earlier novel, *The Last Guru*,[11] Pinkwater satirizes faddish enthusiasm by Westerners for semi-digested bits of Eastern religious and philosophical traditions such as Zen Buddhism. A librarian tells the boys that they are "six or seven years too late" (87). The fad has passed, and all the Zen books have been withdrawn from circulation. The notion of a venerable Oriental tradition first becoming wildly popular, then being abruptly forgotten only a few years later, is a wonderfully telling and only slightly exaggerated portrayal of the fickleness of contemporary American tastes.

The boys' attempts to learn Zen from a cookbook and other popular sources make for some fine comic scenes. "Teach us! Teach us, Master!" they shout to the bewildered Mr. Yee. "We'd seen a couple of kung-fu movies on TV and it was all coming back to us" (92). When Yee mutters to himself, "Where these boys come from?" and "Why they all sit on floor like that?" Charles the Cat informs us, "These questions were the famous Zen koan, which Captain Colossal had read in a Dr. Wizardo comic book" (97).

The interplay of Yee's fractured English with the Ducks' homegrown weirdness is delightful. Many of the misunderstandings between Yee and the Ducks are based upon his Oriental identity. When the boys reverently address him as "Master," he assumes they are making fun of him as a foreigner with a poor grasp of the English language and American culture. Yee's complete unsuitability to be any sort of mentor to the boys—Zen Master or otherwise—is demonstrated by his instinctive fondness for Kevin Shapiro, the Ducks' nemesis and bête noire. Yee's final repudiation of the boys is made all the more bitter when he tells them that gossip provided by Kevin Shapiro is the immediate cause of their dismissal.

Their "Master's" preference for the despised Shapiro is the finale of a series of comic ironies which unfold in rapid succession to doom the Ducks. When they overhear Dr. Cookie Mendoza telling Richard F. Scott (of 5235 Pearl Street)[12] that "there's nothing wrong with masturbating. Everybody does it" (103), they quite naturally suppose that confessing to that practice is going to please the psychiatrist. And indeed, she eggs them on. Naturally, they are stunned when "the treacherous Dr. Cookie Mendoza" (111) then reports them as perverts and recommends harsh discipline. When the Ducks ask Mr. Yee how Kevin Shapiro had known they had been to Dr. Cookie, he replies, "Mr. Shapiro close personal friend of pervert Richard F. Scott, locker room jerk-off artist" (108). Thus, the Ducks are punished for telling Dr. Cookie what she said she wanted to hear: that they engaged in an embarrassing but common and normal practice. Meanwhile, Richard F. Scott, who really *had* been moaning and masturbating in gym lockers, not only escapes punishment by lying, but also provides Mr. Yee—through the envied and despised Shapiro—ammunition for despatching the Ducks.

In his description of Dr. Cookie Mendoza's blatant betrayal of the boys' confidences, Pinkwater depicts an adolescent's worst nightmare. Teenagers can be extremely sensitive about privacy issues, especially where their initial explorations of sexuality are concerned. A high school student might well wonder whether a mental health practitioner employed by the school system could be relied upon to favor the interests of a student "client" over those of her employer, should the two diverge. The black humor encounter of the Ducks with Dr. Mendoza forms an interesting contrast to that of Leonard Neeble with the wacky psychologist Dr. Prince in *Alan Mendelsohn*. Although both incidents are funny, the disastrous outcome of the Ducks' attempt to "snow" Dr. Mendoza makes for a much darker comedy than Leonard Neeble's successful manipulation of Dr. Prince.

The Ducks' parents are equally unsympathetic. The cast of characters of *Young Adult Novel* had been restricted to students and educational staff of Himmler High. The sequel introduces a wider cast, including the worst possible parents for a group of geeky nonconformists. The parents of the Honorable Venustiano Carranza (President of Mexico) tell the Ducks "that we were homosexual devil worshippers, and that God was going to kill us" (95). When the boys get in trouble at school, his parents enroll El Presidente "in the rifle and machine-gun class and Sunday school run by the Anti-Communist White Americans League" (112). Igor's parents "were negotiating with the parish priest to have their son exorcised" (111). Captain Colossal's parents tell him it "was mostly his fault" they were divorcing (112).

These caricatured parents are very funny, but our laughter is a bit edgy. Part of the humor is due to the fact that the behavior of these adults, like that of Dr. Mendoza, is exaggerated in degree, but not in kind. In other words, this is good satire. It hits close enough to home to be grimly recognizable to skeptical adolescents, and a bit uncomfortable for adults. All of the adult characters in *Dead End Dada* condemn, reject, or betray the boys: parents, teachers, principal, psychiatrist, and laundromat owner. These characters may be comic stereotypes, and the situations funny, but there is nevertheless a genuine emotional impact to this tale of persistent rejection.

In fact, after their banishment by "Master" Yee, the boys become sufficiently depressed to consider killing themselves. In the spirit of their adopted Oriental philosophy, El Presidente proposes "honorable ritual suicide" as the appropriate response to their "loss of face" (109).

The boys discuss this option before finally deciding against it. Of course, the episode is relieved by the story's characteristic atmosphere of black comedy. Facetious remarks reassure us that nothing genuinely tragic is going to happen. Nevertheless, the bleak tone of the scene does evoke the very real pathos of teenage suicide.[13] The scene works, as do many scenes in both *Young Adult Novel and Dead End Dada*, by balancing on an ironic ledge, from which it refuses to fall into comedy on one side or tragedy on the other.

Rejection by girls is another problem for the Ducks. *Young Adult Novel* barely mentioned relations between the sexes, beyond a humorous observation that there were no Duckettes. However, *Dead End Dada* contains several sexually-charged references to the boys' lack of success with girls, as well as numerous other sexually explicit remarks and situations.

In addition to the Dr. Mendoza interviews already discussed, there is another hilarious reference to masturbation in *DED*. The boys have gathered at El Presidente's house. They program a VCR to record a TV episode, then program a computer to play both sides of a chess game. "So, with a machine watching television, and another playing with itself, the Dharma Ducks were relieved of having to carry on these two time-consuming activities" (94).

The Ducks' hopeless longing for female companionship is a pervasive theme in the story. The first occurrence is embedded within a statement they compose to mark their change of allegiance from Dada to Zen.

> We are now working for a world cultural revolution, the destruction of authority, freedom for all oppressed peoples, and sex with junior and senior girls, all of them if possible. So far we have failed in our goals, especially the last, but we carry on. . . . We carry condoms in our wallets and look for chances to promote world revolution all the time. (87)

The three gorgeous cheerleaders in constant attendance upon Kevin Shapiro are objects of intense sexual longing and frustration. The boys' reaction to them is reminiscent of Philip Roth's yearning narrator in *Portnoy's Complaint*, or Woody Allen as the bespectacled, overintellectual protagonist in several of Allen's own films. Knowing that these girls are probably vain, frivolous, and socially incompatible with the Ducks doesn't help. They are described as "agonizingly beautiful," and their utter inaccessibility is physically painful.

> Never did the Dharma Ducks see any of these girls without experiencing a shriveling sensation all over, a stab of pain in the crotch, and a realization of our profound worthlessness as human beings . . . our kazoos made a dying sound. (102)

Even Mr. Yee can't help but remark on these spectacular cheerleaders, when he observes to Kevin: "Nice girls with tremendous knockers help you do laundry, yes?" (105).

Pinkwater's handling of sex in *Dead End Dada* is brilliant. Every sexual reference and situation in the narrative—there are perhaps ten in all—is laugh-out-loud funny. Moreover, each of those passages contributes strongly to the effectiveness of the story. The Ducks are accustomed to being reviled by teachers, counselors, and administrators. As Charles the Cat tells us, "frequent purges, political upheavals, and outbreaks of anti- Dada sentiment had resulted in any number of suspensions" (96). They have also become impervious to parental disapproval, as when Charles casually relates, "After our parents had finished yelling at us, abusing us, and threatening us, and after we had had our suppers, we drifted back to the Balkan Falcon Memorial" (106). However, the Ducks' abysmal failure to attract girls cuts much deeper than any of their other difficulties. Being judged potential mate material by a desirable member of the opposite sex is arguably the most essential validation of worthiness for a young person.[14] The Ducks long for that reassurance, and they hope that college will be different.

The Dada Boys in Collitch

The next sequel is nearly the same length, at twenty-four full pages. It has no chapter divisions, being a chapter itself: the formal title of the story is "The first chapter of *The Dada Boys in Collitch*, a novel, to be completed sometime or other" (145). This story, like both previous Dada Boys tales, is narrated by Charles the Cat. He explains to us that he and the Honorable Venustiano Carranza (President of Mexico) have been accepted by a Martwist College in upstate New York.[15] The other three Ducks were not invited to Martwist, but they "simply packed their suitcases and came with us" (145).

The remainder of the story takes place on the campus of Martwist College. Things start well: the five boys are pleasantly surprised to find that they can get away with living in the dormitory room assigned to only two of them. Moreover, the non-matriculated Ducks are not prevented from attending lecture classes, nor from helping themselves to such nourishment as can be obtained from the college cafeteria. But then disappointments and misadventures begin to mount. The Ducks are oppressed by the insanely egotistical and occasionally violent John Holyrood, the "Beast of Nixonn Hall." However, aside from the beastly Holyrood, most of their fellow students seem to be the same sorts of shallow conformists the boys had avoided in high school. They fail to make new friends. Moreover, they are disappointed in their professors and classes. Finally, when Holyrood trashes their room and gets them in trouble with the combined Campus Christian Crusade and Student Court, the boys decide to flee the college. They had previously met a strange old professor in the nearby woods,[16] and they have a vague notion of "hanging out" with him to continue the informal studies they had begun under his tutelage (168). Like both of the earlier Dada Boys chronicles, this story ends with a rueful admission of past failures and a vague hope for better days to come.

Dada Boys in Collitch has its merits, but it is not as strong as the previous two Dada Boys stories. Pinkwater can always be counted upon to deliver good comedy, and this narrative has an acceptable CPC quotient (chortles per chapter.) However, the story does not break as much new ground as did its predecessors. Like *Dead-End Dada*, the story contains humorous passages featuring both sexually explicit material and some general grossness in the *Animal House* mode. The special interest of *Dada Boys in Collitch* lies in its presentation of older protagonists and a college setting.

Judging from this story, Pinkwater is just as ready to satirize college life as that of high school. We meet Professor Brontosaurus, whose orientation lecture features the information that the freshmen can expect to earn "3.6 times more money than we would have earned if we hadn't gone to college." This inspires a lively debate among the Ducks as to whether the three of them who are not officially enrolled will also earn 3.6 times more money. Professor Brontosaurus then tells the assembled freshmen that they could now regard themselves as "better than other people—at least those who hadn't been to college" (149).

We also meet the communications professor, Dr. Horst Whistler, dressed in "a tiny snap-brim hat, pointy shoes, blue jeans, a sleeveless yellow T-shirt with a picture of Twisted Sister on it, and one black glove" (152).

The Ducks then get to know some of their fellow students. There is Ronald Rubin, president of the Business Club, the Pre-Law Club, the Campus Christian Crusade, and so on; and Pulkeh Rabinowitz, who tells Charles, "Someone is going to make his move one of these days and receive the riches of my body." Charles notes that "her other inter-est was folk music" (136).

Sadly, the boys do not last long enough at Martwist to have many experiences with these interesting characters. The Ducks soon become disillusioned with the college's social life and curriculum. When a riot-ous incident involving the Beast of Nixonn Hall and Pulkeh Rabinowitz puts the Ducks in a bad light, they flee the place with few regrets. However, it could be said that they remained at Martwist just long enough to give us a chance to sample Pinkwater's characteristic satiri-cal comedy as applied to a college setting.[17]

The Confessions of Pinkwater by Ken Kelman

Pinkwater has described *Confessions* as "an afterword by Ken Kelman."[18] When asked about the attribution, Pinkwater confirmed that *The Confessions of Pinkwater* was indeed written by Ken Kelman, and not by himself under that pseudonym.[19] Kelman is a long-time friend of Pinkwater, to whom both *The Worms of Kukumlima* and *The Snarkout Boys and the Baconburg Horror* were dedicated. The character, K. E. Kelman, PH (phantomologist) in the latter novel is presumably named after the real Ken Kelman. Several of Pinkwater's autobiographical stories about his bachelor days include anecdotes about Kelman.[20]

Confessions is a bit shorter than either of the Dada Ducks sequels. Although its humorous and surrealistic science fiction atmosphere is reminiscent of some of Pinkwater's writing, *Confessions* has a distinc-tive style. In the story, Pinkwater (Monsieur Eau d'Rouge) dies and arrives at the "Girly Gates." He is unable to enter because he's too heavy. The gatekeeper, "the great dog Trazom" (Mozart) explains that this heaviness is metaphysical; that is, the late author's thoughts are too heavy. A lengthy dialogue ensues, in which Trazom and an unseen voice call upon the ghosts of famous authors quoted in Pinkwater's books, such as Goethe, Mary Shelley, and Voltaire, as witnesses for the prosecution. It is explained that Pinkwater must confess to the heavy ideas expressed in his books before he can become light enough to en-ter. Pinkwater argues vainly that his books had no meaning despite their many intellectual allusions. Ultimately, Pinkwater is grudgingly forced to confess, but he refuses to repent. Instead of becoming lighter, in his pride and defiance he becomes even bigger and heavier, and to the outrage of "the voice," the enormous author expands until he finally breaks the pillars and gates and crashes into Heaven.

Two reviewers of *Young Adults* alluded to *The Confessions of Pinkwater*. Neither raised the issue of authorship, and it appears that both assumed the story was written by Pinkwater himself. According to one reviewer, "The last story (also the weakest) is a bizarre fable in which Pinkwater comments on the meaning of his work."[21] Another observed, "Puns proliferate, but behind the jokes Pinkwater offers a defense of artistic freedom."[22] Knowing that the piece was authored by Ken Kelman, we can partially agree with both critics: in *Confessions*, author Ken Kelman comments on the meaning of his friend's work; and Pinkwater the character in Kelman's story offers a defense of artistic freedom.

Aside from its entertainment value, Kelman's "bizarre fable" does provide valuable insights into Pinkwater's outlook. The supposedly deceased author is made to defend his insistent claim that his books have no message or meaning, against the indisputable evidence that the books are filled with "heavy" cultural references and ideas. Is the author being insincere, or falsely modest, or at least disingenuous, when he makes such denials?

Kelman has hit upon a key aspect of Pinkwater's relationship to his works. The real Daniel Pinkwater has often issued such disclaimers. However, when he insists that his books have no meaning, and that readers are free to make of them whatever they like, what he is really saying is that his books are not didactic; they do not enforce any single meaning. They are indeed filled with references to popular and classical culture. At their best they are rich and allusive, offering a great deal of meaning to readers of all ages and types. But the significance, what one "gets" from a Pinkwater novel, will vary with each reader. There is no "message," no single correct interpretation, and no moral lesson.[23]

In *Confessions*, Pinkwater's "defense of artistic freedom" is successful. Refusing to repent and thereby reduce himself so he can fit between the Girly Gates, he defiantly insists that he is glad to have written everything he did. To the consternation of the gatekeepers, the swelling of his pride enables the enormous author to crash the gates of heaven in a manner not forseen by the angels. "And he expanded and broke the pillars and the gates came crashing down, and he rolled into a vision of emerald and sapphire and peaches and cream" (224). Greatness trumps smallness. As in Dickens' *A Christmas Carol*, generosity and expansiveness triumph over mean, petty narrowness. "'The clouds are whipped cream!' shrieked Pinkwater. 'Oh, see, flan, tutti frutti!'" (224). To this delirious finale, we can but cheer, "Roll to glory, big guy!"

NOTES

1. Pinkwater is a talented cartoonist. *Norb*, a comic strip he co-authored with Tony Auth, although short-lived, is fondly remembered by many fans. During the mid-1980s, Pinkwater illustrated several of his children's books with the same Macintosh-produced cartoon technique: *Jolly Roger, a Dog of Hoboken* (1985), and *The Muffin Fiend*, *The Frankenbagel Monster*, and *The Moosepire* (all 1986).
2. However, there may be a short story collection on the horizon. *"Uncle Boris in the Yukon, or, The Kootenai Yid,"* will be included in a collection of short stories to be published by Simon and Schuster more than a year from now." *The (Sort of) Official Daniel Pinkwater Website, Talk to DP Forum, Archive*, 1 *<http://www.designfoundry.com/p-zone>* (27 November 1999).
3. *Kliatt Young Adult Paperback Guide* (winter 1986), 31.
4. However, one of Pinkwater's picture books, *Devil in the Drain* (New York: Dutton, 1984) was challenged in the Galesville-Ettrick, Wisconsin School District in 1987. Robert P. Doyle, *Banned Books 1999 Resource Guide* (Chicago: American Library Association, 1999), 77.
5. Michael Dirda, *Washington Post Book World* (1 December 1985): 11.
6. Lechner, 18.
7. *Kliatt Young Adult Paperback Guide* (winter 1986): 31.
8. Daniel Pinkwater, *Young Adults* (New York: Tom Doherty Associates, 1985), 78.
9. This is not to imply any disrespect for the real Lieutenant Onada, a brave soldier whose stubbornness was as magnificent as it was excessive. Hiroo Onada, *No Surrender: My Thirty-year War*, translated into English by Charles S. Terry. (Annapolis: Naval Institute Press, 1999).
10. The name is funny not only because of the unlikely combination of the given name Sigmund with a Chinese surname, but also because of the allusion—in context of the boys' questionable sanity—to Sigmund Freud, and finally because it sounds like that of Syngman Rhee, president of the Republic of Korea, 1948-1960. All-in-all, it's an ironically powerful and resonant name for such a dull character.
11. Daniel Pinkwater, *The Last Guru* (New York: Dodd, Mead, 1978).
12. The Ducks know Richard F. Scott's exact name and address because while sitting in Dr. Mendoza's waiting room, they could clearly overhear every word of her "confidential" interview with Richard.
13. The tone is reminiscent of Bud Cort's fake suicides in the cult film *Harold and Maude* (1971).
14. Certainly in strict biological terms this is so; absent the acceptance of mates by its young adults, a species will soon cease to exist!
15. Martwist College does not exist. However, Pinkwater himself is a graduate of Bard College, in upstate New York.
16. This character introduces himself as Heinrich Bleucher. A German philosopher (and husband of Hannah Arendt) named Heinrich Bluecher taught at Bard College after fleeing Nazi Europe c. 1940. Pinkwater told this author that

he knew and liked Professor Bluecher. Email from D. Pinkwater to W. Hogan, 9 December 1999.
17. When asked if he had run into any professors like Prof. Brontosaurus or Dr. Horst Whistler during his own college days, Pinkwater replied, "Certainly not at Bard College. I was happy as a bird there—and about as likely to become educated, for which I do not blame the college. I had a single semester of college teaching, (one class only), at an institution I will not name, which gave me all the material I needed for the institution the dada boys attended." Email from D. Pinkwater to W. Hogan, 9 December 1999.
18. *Talk to DP Forum, Archive*, 10 (1 December 1999).
19. Email communication from D. Pinkwater to W. Hogan, 2 December 1999. Pinkwater helped this author to contact Kelman, who sounded on the phone exactly as Pinkwater has described him: "My friend Ken Kelman is a genius—a playwright and film critic. He's lived his whole life in Manhattan . . . What he did, mainly, was sit in dark theaters." Daniel Pinkwater, *Hoboken Fish and Chicago Whistle* (Princeton, N.J.: Xlibris, 1999), 46. Kelman comes across rather like Woody Allen.
20. *Hoboken Fish*, 46-53, 299, 378-80.
21. *Kliatt Young Adult Paperback Guide* (winter 1986): 31.
22. Dirda, 11.
23. Pinkwater expressed this eloquently in a response he posted to a fan on the Web: "As far as containing a message, let alone wisdom, or any kind of subtext, I deny that they [my stories] do . . . or if they do, it's by accident, and not my fault. Most probably you're experiencing the effect of any well-executed work of art, that is, it has an inner organization that may concentrate your mind, which is probably why it gives pleasure. Thus concentrated, you begin to see how things relate, and attribute meaning and intent the work of art may not have." *Talk to DP Forum*, 21 (8 August 1999). Wow. The man should be teaching aesthetics. Or maybe he is.

Chapter 10

The Education of Robert Nifkin

Following *Young Adults* in 1985, Pinkwater brought out no further young adult novel until *The Education of Robert Nifkin*, in 1998. During those thirteen years, Pinkwater published over twenty picture books, but only one other novel for young readers, *Borgel*, in 1990.

If we divide Pinkwater's writing career into two equal halves, his shift away from children's novels becomes quite noticeable. During his first decade and a half as an author, 1970-1985, Pinkwater's publications included:

- nineteen picture books
- eleven novels for the pre-adolescent, or mid-grade audience
- five young adult novels
- one non-fiction book

During the next fifteen years, 1986-2000, Pinkwater published:

- twenty-eight picture books
- one novel for the pre-adolescent audience (*Borgel*)
- one young adult novel (*The Education of Robert Nifkin*)
- one adult novel (*The Afterlife Diet*)
- two collections of essays, many adapted from NPR broadcasts[1]

It is evident that while Pinkwater has increased his already prolific output of illustrated books for young children, his production of novels fell off quite dramatically after 1985: sixteen before and only three after. When asked about this phenomenon, Pinkwater replied:

> For quite a while, editors with whom I dealt desired to please their masters by publishing picture books, which were understood—rightly or wrongly—to have the potential of earning more money than novels. Once the industry gets hold of some formula, (no matter that it

may be pure superstition), it tends to be pervasive, and hard to shake. Of course, novels have been published all the while, but in my case—that of a writer who can do short books as well—it was easy to steer me. These days, in the aftermath of Harry Potter, I expect longer books will make a strong comeback. This is a good thing.[2]

Those of us who love Pinkwater's novels certainly hope that such a shift in the marketplace will increase both the readership of his completed novels and the author's incentives to write more of them in the future. But, even before the success of J. K. Rowling's Harry Potter novels, Pinkwater's *The Education of Robert Nifkin* was quite well received by the critics in 1998. All of the journals regularly reviewing juvenile literature had kind words for *Robert Nifkin*. It was described as a "very funny book,"[3] a "toothy satire,"[4] a "funny, over-the-top satire,"[5] "a treat to read,"[6] and "a good choice for the teen collection."[7]

Several reviewers commented on Pinkwater's vivid lampooning of high school life: "the novel literally crackles and the comedy is occasionally laugh-out-loud funny as Pinkwater takes potshots at the 'wonderful' high school years."[8] "Right down at the other end of the alley from earnestly p.c. high school sagas, this book will find its way to the hearts of individualists everywhere."[9] "Pinkwater fans should appreciate the anarchy as well as the irreverent descriptions of high school life."[10]

In addition, the novel was included in a short list of recommended summer reading for youth in *USA Today*. That article described *Robert Nifkin* as "a very funny account of an anarchic Chicago adolescence."[11]

Upon opening the book, before reaching the story proper, one finds a curious unnumbered prefatory page containing a brief entry purporting to be a line or two from page four of a college admission application form:

> 64. Characterize, in essay form, your high-school experience.
> You may use additional sheets of paper as needed.[12]

There are no further references to college admissions until the very end of the book.

As the story begins, it is quickly evident from certain cultural references that the time period of *The Education of Robert Nifkin* is the 1950s. The narrator, Robert Nifkin, must begin high school in a new town where he has no friends. Riverview High School, in suburban Chicago, is understood to be a fairly typical American public school, or at any rate typical of that institution as portrayed in many of Daniel

Pinkwater's novels. That is to say, most of Riverview's students are shallow conformists, and most of its teachers and administrators either petty martinettes or time-serving dullards.

Robert soon comes to hate Riverview. Finally, one morning he finds himself unable to get off his bus at the school stop, and he rides onward. Robert begins skipping school most days, sometimes to sample Chicago's cultural attractions by himself, and sometimes to help his new friend, Riverview dropout Kenny Papescu, with odd jobs. The school bureaucracy takes several months to catch up with Robert, but finally his truancy and academic failure are revealed, and he is assigned to a tough reform school.

Fortunately for Robert, he had been introduced by Kenny to an eccentric private school, which he could propose to his parents in lieu of reform school. As Robert eloquently puts it, "My ass was saved" (119). Robert is duly matriculated into the Wheaton School, an extremely laissez-faire institution, where such petty concerns as class attendance are never allowed to shackle the free spirits of a happy community of nonconformist teachers and students. Robert thrives in this environment, and after an initial period of goofing off, finds unconventional but effective teachers who encourage genuine learning. College even becomes a possibility.

At the very end of the novel, we are reminded that the entire narrative is Robert's college admissions essay. We had been told this at the book's beginning, but most readers will have long since forgotten that this 168-page narrative is supposed to be a teenager's response to item #64 on a standard form. "Use additional sheets of paper as needed"—indeed! Robert concludes,

> And I am happy—or I will be when I know for sure that I am going to be allowed to continue my education in a fine and venerable institution like St. Leon's College.
> This essay is respectfully submitted by:
Robert Nifkin, Chicago, October 1958 (168)

This date underscores the autobiographical character of the novel: Daniel Pinkwater was born in 1941, and he probably applied to college himself in the fall of 1958, at the start of his own senior year in high school.

Familiarity with Pinkwater's previous young adult novels is an important determinant of one's probable reaction to *Robert Nifkin*. Admirers of Pinkwater's earlier books are more likely to smile with fond recognition than to laugh out loud with surprise at most of *Robert Nifkin's* humorous episodes.

The Education of Robert Nifkin is the epitome of a Daniel Pinkwater novel. There is nothing entirely new; nearly all of the characters and situations are variations on familiar Pinkwater themes, but they're especially well-handled here. There is a mature balance to the novel. The reader senses the deft touch of a master who has developed ease and confidence with his materials after decades of steady application to his craft. Other Pinkwater novels contain wilder heights of imaginative fancy, more laugh-out-loud moments, and sharper satire than *Robert Nifkin*. But none of his books are more fully representative of the whole range of Pinkwater's art and philosophy than *The Education of Robert Nifkin*.

Although it reprises many of Pinkwater's previous novels, *Robert Nifkin* bears a special relationship to one earlier novel in particular. To fully appreciate this connection, let us consider the following plot: A geeky, overweight Jewish boy moves with his parents to a new neighborhood. He has no siblings, and finds no friends in the sterile new neighborhood. His parents are content with their tacky redecorating projects, but he is miserable. Not being good-looking, fashionably dressed, or athletic, he becomes an instant outcast at his new school. The principal and teachers, besides being mediocre educators, are anti-intellectual, anti-Semitic, homophobic, red-baiting McCarthyites. The regular gym teacher is a fascist brute, but fortunately, our narrator is able to enroll in an alternative gym class. Our narrator hates school, and he is soon flunking all of his classes even though he's quite intelligent. He plays hooky at every opportunity, and has far more meaningful and educational experiences outside of school than within it. He loves riding his morning bus right past the school bus stop and continuing on for weekday adventures in the city. He finds interesting food in local restaurants, in contrast to the poor fare cooked by his mother.

His life takes a crucial turn for the better when he makes friends with an unusual boy of about his own age. In contrast to our narrator, who has a penchant for bumbling straight into disasters, this new friend has terrific street smarts and is skilled at manipulating people and institutions to his advantage, in a benign way, which does no real harm to anyone. With his new friend, our narrator encounters a variety of eccentrics and con artists who contribute to his practical education. He begins to emerge from boredom, truancy, and depression. By the end of the story, the helpful friend is no longer needed; the narrator has developed his own survival skills and is clearly on his way to a successful life.

Which of Pinkwater's novels fits that plot description? The correct answer is two of them: Pinkwater's first young adult novel, *Alan Mendelsohn, the Boy from Mars*, and his latest, *The Education of Robert Nifkin*. It would not be much of an exaggeration to say that *Robert Nifkin* is a reworking of *Alan Mendelsohn*, two decades later.

So how can *Robert Nifkin* occupy a place of high honor in the Pinkwater canon if it is "just" a reworking of *Alan Mendelsohn*? Well, it's far from being *just* that. For starters, the simplified plot description above slurred over some significant differences between the two books. Mr. Nifkin—clearly modeled on Pinkwater's own father—is a much tougher, earthier, and far more interesting character than the colorless Mr. Neeble. Kenny Papescu is nothing like Alan Mendelsohn; he's older, a street-smart hustler, and exhibits no exotic behavior, let alone a Martian ancestry. Robert Nifkin's escape from Riverview to a very different sort of school contrasts with Leonard Neeble's return to the same public school, after he had developed some coping mechanisms. The strong, nostalgic 1950s feel of *Robert Nifkin*, featuring rich, summer nighttime forays to the Clark (Snark) Theater and other Chicago destinations bears closer similarity to the atmosphere of the Snarkout novels than to that of *Alan Mendelsohn*.

The most obvious and profound departure is the total absence of science fiction/fantasy elements in *Robert Nifkin*. Whereas the earlier novel had resorted to a *deus ex machina* "boy from Mars" as Leonard Neeble's guardian angel, Robert's "saviors" in *Robert Nifkin* are the very earthbound characters, Linda Pudovkin and Kenny Papescu. Whereas Leonard's rite of passage occurred in the "alternate world" of Waka-Waka, the places where Robert Nifkin matures are all very prosaic (some are, or were actual) locales in the city of Chicago. In place of the paranormal "mind control techniques" practiced by Leonard and Alan, Robert gains mastery through his own efforts and by following some good mentors. All of this is entirely realistic and plausible. *Alan Mendelsohn* is often classified as science fiction, but no one would consider placing *Robert Nifkin* in that category. The fact that the two books are so much alike in spite of such a categorical distinction is evidence of the genre-defying nature of much of Daniel Pinkwater's work.

The essential point we should appreciate is that Pinkwater can tell the same type of story, with the same themes, whether he uses science fiction or not. His very early novel, *Wingman* (1975), embodies this dual potentiality. *Wingman* has a great deal in common with both *Alan Mendelsohn* and with *Robert Nifkin*. Like those later novels, it is essentially the story of a boy's salvation from truancy, failure, and depression, when he finds good mentors who enable him to build on his strengths and to succeed in spite of an apathetic school organization.

Donald Chen, the protagonist of *Wingman*, finds two mentors: the fantastic Wingman, and the very human Mrs. Miller, a warm and sympathetic substitute teacher. At least one critic commented that the superhero character, Wingman, is the weakest element of that novel, and that his presence perhaps even detracts.[13] Without taking up that argument, it is sufficient for us to note that the essential story, *Wingman*, whose very title, like that of *Alan Mendelsohn, the Boy from Mars*, is named for a science fiction character, could easily be retold without its overt science fiction content. With *Robert Nifkin*, Pinkwater actually carried out such an experiment, writing a novel that is, among other things, a retelling of *Alan Mendelsohn* without the science fiction.

In Pinkwater's fictional world, the normal can be nearly as fantastic and wonderful as the paranormal. There is no sharp boundary between Pinkwater's comically exaggerated, but essentially realistic characters—for example the outrageously bad teachers and psychologists who populate many of Pinkwater's stories—and his explicitly supernatural characters such as Alan Mendelsohn or Wingman.

The element of wonder in *The Education of Robert Nifkin* is supplied not by science fiction, but rather by exuberant leaps of fancy, which however exaggerated, break no physical laws. There are some enjoyable examples in *Nifkin*, including the grossly expensive and tacky residence of Miles Greenthorpe, and the faux antiques sold by Kenny Papescu and his father to gullible nouveau riche clients. These include a polyurethane-protected table painting attributed to the fifteenth-century artist Heironymus Bosch, and a desk which "might have belonged to Sigmund Freud" (40).

Pinkwater's world is also filled with wonderful places that have a dreamlike quality of being almost but not quite real, such as Tintown and Beanbender's Beer Garden in *The Snarkout Boys and the Avocado of Death*, and Riverview High School in *Nifkin*. These places are surreal rather than unreal. That is, they are composed of ordinary elements, which have been idealized or caricatured. Sometimes the elements seem to have been rearranged as if by the subconscious imagination during a dream or a nostalgic daydream. Science fiction is simply one of Pinkwater's tools. His novels are fantastic in every sense of that word whether or not they include overtly paranormal phenomena.

Returning to the comparison of *Alan Mendelsohn* with *Robert Nifkin*, the age of the characters, and their consequent interests, are quite different. The protagonist of the earlier novel is in his first year of junior high school, and that book contains no sexual remarks or situations. However, as we follow Robert Nifkin through his high school years, we do encounter, appropriately, some more mature situations, including some mild sexual content.[14]

As we noted in chapters 8 and 9, Pinkwater demonstrated a deft touch with sexual humor in *Young Adult Novel* and *Young Adults*. The same fine handling of comic sexual situations is evident in *The Education of Robert Nifkin*. Most of these episodes are quite understated, for example the sly references to Miss Roanoke, who "was regularly called in for consultations" with the school's benefactor (131). A passage mentioning the new students at Wheaton is also nicely put: "Each of them would make his or her contribution to the life of our little school. Janice Steinway, a tall blond freshman, attracted a lot of attention, as she appeared to be especially willing to contribute (166).

Such passages illustrate both Pinkwater's overall skill as a humorist, and his versatility in properly calibrating that humor to the age of his narrator and intended audience; here, the upper end of the young adult population.

Another major theme of the book, that of learning, is at the heart of many of Pinkwater's novels. However, in none of them is it more central than in *The Education of Robert Nifkin*, whose very title explicitly states the book's main subject. Robert finds he is unable to gain an education at Riverview High School. Like Leonard Neeble and Walter Galt and the Dada Ducks, he is unwilling or unable to join the herd, to fit in with the mass of high school students who drift mindlessly through the numbing hours of enforced attendance in a mediocre public school.

In *Alan Mendelsohn*, Leonard Neeble learned how to cope. In the two Snarkout novels, Walter, Winston, and Rat endured their uninspiring schools with cynical wit, and were sustained by their rich extracurricular adventures. The Dada Boys forever sought enlightenment, but were never able to find it. Despairing of Dada, Zen, and a cult of W. A. Mozart in turn, they were last seen in the unpromising pursuit of yet another guru, an eccentric old man who appeared to them in the woods, claiming to be a leprechaun and bearing the name of a former German philosophy professor.

The Education of Robert Nifkin, unlike those earlier novels, presents a young narrator who actually manages to obtain the rough equivalent of a high school education. However, Robert's path to knowledge is quite unconventional. After flunking out of his local public high school, Robert finds himself at the Wheaton School, obviously a pretty wild place.

When my mother and I came for my application/entrance inter-
view/acceptance to the Wheaton School, the first thing we saw was a
body falling from an upper floor, down through the repeated oval of
that staircase, and thudding to the marble floor. This was followed by
a cheer. (121)

Uncertain whether the Wheaton School was really intended to appear as disorderly as it seemed, this author asked Daniel Pinkwater if
we should conceive of the place as being in the mold of those liberal
academies founded upon the educational theories of Maria Montessori
or Rudolf Steiner.[15] Pinkwater replied,

The Wheaton School is not a bit like a Montessori or Rudolf Steiner
school, in that there's no philosophy or intention behind it—it's
chaos, and a swindle for most of the students. It works as a school for
some of the kids entirely circumstantially.[16]

Although Robert does manage to find some good teacher/mentors
there, Pinkwater further clarified that in *Robert Nifkin*, "My 'good'
teachers are good for bad, or unprepared, or previously shortchanged
students. It's possible that a kid with a better prior education might
need a different kind of good teacher."[17]

So, although we have finally witnessed an adolescent Pinkwater
character in the process of acquiring a decent education, we cannot say
that the Wheaton School represents Pinkwater's prescription for a good
academy, nor that Wally Gershkowitz is Pinkwater's general model of
a good teacher. They happened to work for Robert Nifkin. When asked
what a good high school might be like, Pinkwater replied,

If Robert Nifkin were a real person, instead of a character in a novel,
I might wish something like this for him: He is recruited by a progressive college, or a progressive program within a conventional
college, which provides him with a suggested syllabus, and possibly a
pre-college advisor he may contact at lengthy intervals. After a
minimum one year of unsupervised study, he can apply to take an
entrance exam. He can take the exam as often as he likes—it changes
and becomes more complex each time. Conceivably, a non-
matriculate would be able to flunk the exam enough times that he
would be offered a degree, instantly, the first time he passes it.[18]

There are at least two points of special interest in Pinkwater's remark. First, the absence of any expressed concern for the social aspects of high school life—football games, cheerleaders, pep rallies, proms, school songs, letter sweaters, and all the other paraphernalia and traditions of the American high school. Pinkwater never refers to that side of high school life other than ironically. A passage from his tongue-in-cheek preface to *Young Adults* is apposite:

> It is this author's devout hope that in time he may be able to produce acceptable books about cute furry animals and—for the older reader—stories about high schools in California with really good athletic programs and uniformly attractive students."[19]

The other element that comes through clearly is Pinkwater's emphasis upon self-learning. We all hope to find good teachers. However, we are each responsible for educating ourselves, whether we manage to find good schools and good teachers or not.

> My high school experiences, pretty realistically characterized in the book, [*Nifkin*] were abysmal. All I learned was that authority figures are usually stupid, and easily evaded, and that I was capable of feeding my own head. Every time I've written about a bad school, I am surprised and dismayed by the number of people who respond, saying I've depicted their own experience.[20]

Clearly, Pinkwater cares deeply about learning. Just as clearly, his conception of a learning environment is not anchored upon the formal school setting. Neither the social ambience nor the curricula of our educational institutions are guaranteed to provide for any of a young person's real needs. Good teachers and mentors are essential, but in Pinkwater's novels they are found in surprising places, and usually not in the front of a classroom.

Nifkin features some of Pinkwater's finest teacher portraits. The "good" teacher and mentor at Wheaton, Wally Gershkowitz, is quite a character, with some very creative educational techniques. But he is relatively normal in comparison with Riverview's wonderful Mrs. Kukla. The fractured diction of this high school English teacher is a delight. On Robert's first full day at Riverview, her welcoming speech begins with horrible grammar, "This is your homcroom which it's the place you come first every day," and ends with the lovely malapropism, "If anybody gives you Communist propaganda or pornography I want to see it" (49).

The Education of Robert Nifkin, coming on the heels of *5 Novels*, put Daniel Pinkwater's name (and face!—on the cover of the latter) prominently on the juvenile racks of bookstores across the country. Along with reprints of *The Hoboken Chicken Emergency* and several other early novels, Pinkwater ended the century with a smashing return to prominence in the adolescent and pre-adolescent market, to complement his perennial strength in the picture book category.

NOTES

1. The above totals include only first editions of new material. Many of Pinkwater's books have been reprinted, and in some cases, the reprints have varied from the original. For example, the 1999 paperback reprint of *The Hoboken Chicken Emergency* features new illustrations by Jill Pinkwater. Since no reprints or variant editions were counted here, the resulting total of sixty-nine titles is the most conservative possible count of Pinkwater's books.
2. Email from D. Pinkwater to W. Hogan, 10 January 2000.
3. *Horn Book Guide* (Jan-June 1998): 347.
4. *Kirkus Reviews* (15 April 1998): 585
5. *Publisher's Weekly* (23 March 1998): 101.
6. Paula Rohrlick, *Kliatt Young Adult Paperback Book Guide* (July 1998): 8.
7. *Children's Book Review Service* (May 1998): 120.
8. Stephanie Zwirin, *Booklist* (1 June 1998): 1749.
9. *Horn Book Magazine* (July/August 1998): 495.
10. John Sigwald, *School Library Journal* (July 1998): 98.
11. Linda Mallon, "Summer Reading List Colored by Blush of Youth," *USA Today* (2 July 1998): D.5.
12. Daniel Pinkwater, *The Education of Robert Nifkin* (New York: Farrar, Strauss, Giroux, 1998); hereafter cited in text as *Nifkin*.
13. "Unfortunately, this Chinese Superman does not quite come off as the splendid character he could have been, and the part of the story dealing with Wingman's flights cruises on leaden wings. The problem, perhaps, is the difficulty of injecting a fantastic element into a real and touching situation." Jane Geniesse, "Wingman," *New York Times Book Review* (4 May 1975): 40. For the opposing view, see Michelle Landsberg, *Reading for the Love of It* (New York: Prentice-Hall, 1986), 68, who argues strongly in favor of the character's utility in the story.
14. However, what is hilariously *inappropriate* about these passages is the notion that Robert would actually dare to include anecdotes of a sexual nature on his college admissions form—especially when one recalls that the entire novel is supposed to be his application essay to a denominational college, St. Leon's.
15. Schools founded upon the respective philosophies of European educators Maria Montessori (1870-1952) and Rudolf Steiner (1861-1925) continue to thrive.

16. Email from D. Pinkwater to W. Hogan, 18 January 2000.
17. Email from D. Pinkwater to W. Hogan, 18 January 2000.
18. Email from D. Pinkwater to W. Hogan, 18 January 2000.
19. *Young Adults*, 83.
20. Email from D. Pinkwater to W. Hogan, 18 January 2000.

Chapter 11

Menippus, Keats, Pinkwater, and the "Big A"

Let us imagine for a moment that we have spent years collecting first editions of every one of Daniel Pinkwater's books of fiction published through the year 2000. Many are now out of print, but we have persevered, and at last we have them all. Now, how to display this extraordinary and valuable collection? We clear a few shelves and then we arrange the books chronologically, from *The Terrible Roar* (1970) to *The Magic Pretzel* (2000). Interesting, but perhaps not the most useful arrangement. So we reorganize them alphabetically by title, from *Alan Mendelsohn* through *Young Larry*. Now it's easy to find any title, but it seems too much like an official library collection, so we experiment with some other arrangements—by color, by height, and so on.

Since, as devotees of an author like Daniel Pinkwater we're naturally very creative persons, we also try some more subtle and esoteric combinations. We organize the books by series—Snarkouts here, Blue Moose books there, and so on. Then we arrange them by topic: books about giant chickens, books about werewolves and vampires, books about characters with obsessive compulsive behaviors—now we're cooking! We've got Uncle Melvin, who says he can make it rain by turning to the left, and cause rainbows by turning to the right.[1] Lunchbox Louie, who feels compelled to bring home a larger animal each day to show his wife, Bigfoot the Chipmunk, and his son, King Waffle, how much their kitten, Wuggie Norple has grown.[2] Mr. Galt, who introduces avocados into every conversation.[3] Steve Nickelson, who is fanatically devoted to health food: "You can't work with inferior materials. That's why the olive milk shake I invented last month was a failure—I used canned olives."[4]

Well, that was much more entertaining, but restless intellectuals that we are, we soon become bored with linear arrangements. Just as a solitaire player will eventually grow weary of laying cards flat on a table and will try building a house of cards, we decide to assemble Pinkwater's books into an architectural monument with those for older readers at the top. How will it come out? We have no trouble building a solid foundation from Pinkwater's fifty-plus picture books. We can construct additional "stories" from those that seem to have been written for older children. Then we can add a level composed of his eleven middle-grade works, and a narrower and even higher level of his half dozen books for young adults. This pyramid of fiction for successively more mature audiences could be capped with the author's single novel for the adult market, *The Afterlife Diet*.

Before our pyramid of books comes tumbling down, let's consider whether that tapering distribution suggests anything about Pinkwater's standing as an author of young adult fiction. Should he be viewed as primarily a writer of books for grade schoolers, who only occasionally writes the "odd" young adult novel? Not at all. The recent publication of his fine young adult novel, *The Education of Robert Nifkin*, demonstrates that Pinkwater remains an important creator of fiction for adolescents. As the author has explained on numerous occasions, his reduced output of novels since the mid-1980s has been due to the requirements of his publishers rather than to his own inclinations. It is to be hoped that those who publish Pinkwater's books will anticipate a market for more of the author's longer fiction. As Pinkwater told a fan who pleaded for another Dada Boys novel, "You don't understand—I can write the book. I can write any number of books. The question is, 'will anybody publish it?' I can't afford to write things I can't place with publishers."[5]

Pinkwater's half dozen books for young adults could be said to consist of three pairs. There are two formal sequences: *The Snarkout Boys and the Avocado of Death*, with its sequel, *The Snarkout Boys and the Baconburg Horror*; and *Young Adult Novel*, with its sequel, *Young Adults*. Finally, as explained in the previous chapter, *The Education of Robert Nifkin* is in some important respects a reprise of *Alan Mendelsohn, the Boy from Mars*, without the science fiction and fantasy trappings of that earlier novel. Those five novels, along with the stories contained in *Young Adults*, represent a significant body of fiction for adolescents. If Pinkwater had written nothing but those six books, he would still be an important author. Fortunately for his readers, the actual extent of Pinkwater's fictional universe is far richer. For each one of his half-dozen young adult books, the author has produced ten additional works of fiction. Many of those picture books, illustrated stories, and novels for pre-adolescents offer similar reading pleasures to those found in Pinkwater's young adult books.

The subject matter of Pinkwater's fictional universe is extremely varied, but certain themes recur throughout his work, across all readership categories. These include a fascination with food and fatness; sympathy for outsiders and underdogs;[6] a celebration of urban neighborhoods, vintage architecture, and other "dying cultural treasures;"[7] an insistence upon independent thinking and self-education; and advocacy of the joy of using one's imagination to discover magic in everyday life. His favorite satirical targets are pompous would-be arbiters of taste, culture, and education. From his briefest picture books to his full-length novels, Pinkwater's heroes are good parents and educators who encourage young people to develop their minds and imaginations. His worst villains are those parents and educators who stifle young minds.

All of Pinkwater's books are characterized by clear prose. There is never any misunderstanding as to what is occurring or being described in his books. There may be fantasy, science fiction, strange characters and frenzied activity, but the descriptions and dialogues are rendered with absolute clarity. Narration is always either first person, or else a basic third person viewpoint from immediately behind the protagonist. *The Hoboken Chicken Emergency* and *The Snarkout Boys and the Baconburg Horror* are exceptional in presenting multiple narrative viewpoints, including newspaper and radio/tv broadcast transcripts, and *Borgel* includes one chapter with an alternate perspective. However, on the whole Pinkwater's narrative technique is extremely plain. The low-key, understated style of his prose creates an effective setting for the eccentric characters and unusual situations that are described.

Pinkwater has said that he likes to put ordinary characters into unusual situations, citing a scene from *Borgel*: "In one of my novels, there is a scene in which people are riding in an old car, through time and space, eating fig bars. Somehow, it's the fig bars that make it believable."[8] We should add that Pinkwater also does exactly the opposite: he will drop exotic characters like Attila the Hun, or fat men from space, or a two hundred and sixty-six pound chicken into a residential neighborhood of Hoboken, New Jersey, or some such mundane setting. These storytelling practices are common to all of Pinkwater's fictional works.

How, then, do Pinkwater's young adult novels and stories fit within his overall body of work? Do they present the same kinds of characters, plot structures, and themes as his books for younger readers? Do they vary only in the use of more mature language and situations, or are they qualitatively different from his works for children?

Let us first consider the most obvious markers of "mature" content—violence, sex, and profanity. None of Pinkwater's books contain any violence whatever, aside from the sort of pratfalls and lumps on the head that occur in Laurel and Hardy films.[9] And although Pinkwater populates his books for all readership levels with fictional monsters, those monsters are quite benign, usually comical, and there is nothing approaching genuine horror in any of the author's stories. Not a drop of blood is spilled, and no serious injuries are sustained by anyone, despite the presence of phantoms, vampires, and extraterrestrials, all running amok in an atmosphere of comic pandemonium.

Some of Pinkwater's young adult books include sexual content. *Young Adults* is by far the most sexually explicit. The first of its two original stories, *Dead End Dada*, contains numerous references to masturbation and to the hopeless lusts of the Dada Ducks. The second, *Dada Boys in Collitch*, presents a rowdy bedroom scene in addition to some sexual dialogue and innuendo. Two others, *The Education of Robert Nifkin* and *Young Adult Novel*, each include some sexual references, but these are less overt than the passages in *Young Adults*. Pinkwater's remaining young adult works—*Alan Mendelsohn* and the two Snarkout novels—are quite innocent, with only some passing references to relations between the sexes, such as Rat's fanatical devotion to the memory of James Dean.

As for profanity, the notorious opening sentence of *Robert Nifkin*, "My father is a son-of-a-bitch from Eastern Europe,"[10] immediately sets that novel apart from Pinkwater's other writings for youthful readers. *The Education of Robert Nifkin* includes perhaps as many as ten occurrences of profanity. Pinkwater's protagonists and narrators usually speak plain conversational English, without profanity or even slang. The dialogue of Pinkwater's young characters is sharp and clever, and comes across as convincing adolescent speech. However, the realism and effectiveness of these passages are achieved through wit, delivery, and content, rather than through any specialized vocabulary.

Some of the differences between Pinkwater's books for young adults and those he has written for children are exactly as one would expect from any author writing for each of those respective audiences. The young adult novels tend to be lengthier and to contain more complex language and concepts than do the picture books and most of the middle-grade stories.[11]

Like most children's authors, Pinkwater populates his books with characters of about the same age as his target audience. Thus, his picture books often center on young children,[12] while his intermediate books feature youths aged about nine to eleven. All of Pinkwater's young adult books are narrated by and are chiefly concerned with adolescents. Whether his young characters are fully developed, like Robert Nifkin; or flat and stereotyped, like the Wild Dada Ducks, they all behave in age-appropriate ways. The youngest are naïve, unselfconscious, and dependent upon their parents; while the teenagers are worldly, image-conscious, and rebellious. Quite a few of the adults in Pinkwater's books are outrageously vain, foolish, and immature, but that's another matter![13]

Aside from these expected variations, there are some distinctive characteristics of Pinkwater's books for each of the various age groups. Many of his books for younger readers have science fiction themes, and most also have important animal characters.[14] However, among his young adult works, only *Alan Mendelsohn*, Pinkwater's first and transitional young adult novel, has an outer space theme.[15] Animals are not central in any of the young adult novels.[16]

The public school experience, so crucial to all of the young adult books, is a much less vital element of Pinkwater's other fiction. Several of his picture books focus upon the classroom (notably, *Author's Day*, *Second Grade Ape*, and the Potato Kids series), but among his eleven intermediate books, only the earliest, *Wingman*, has an important school component. Nearly all of the intermediate books take place while the protagonist is on vacation from school.

Pinkwater's young adult novels have a higher ratio of interesting female characters than do his other fictional works. Rat (a.k.a. Harrison Saunders Bentley Matthews) is a young woman with an attitude. Her strong personality enlivens both Snarkout novels. *The Education of Robert Nifkin* is enriched by the presence of both Pamela Greenthorpe and Linda Pudovkin, two enjoyably quirky teenagers.

Pinkwater's other three young adult books lack genuine women or girl characters. Dr. Cookie Mendoza of *Dead End Dada*, and Pulkeh Rabinowitz of *Dada Boys in Collitch* are excellent comic figures, but not real personalities. Nevertheless, the presence within a good half of his young adult books of strong female characters contrasts with the nearly complete absence of such characters in Pinkwater's intermediate fiction. Among those eleven works, only *Wingman* includes a woman character that is essential to the book's plot. Mrs. Miller plays a vital role in that story, however she is a rather stereotypical "good" teacher and not a vivid or unique personality. Of course, full character development is not always possible within a short work of fiction such as *Wingman* (sixty-three pages), but Pinkwater's several novel-length books for pre-adolescents also lack female characters.

All of the young adult novels and stories have a strong "buddy" element: Leonard Neeble has Alan Mendelsohn, Walter Galt has Winston Bongo and Rat, Robert Nifkin has Kenny Papescu, and the outcast Wild Dada Ducks have each other (no one else will have anything to do with them!). These sorts of vital friendships are not often featured in Pinkwater's fiction for younger children. A few of his picture books are based on important peer relationships, notably *Doodle Flute* and *Spaceburger*, the two Kevin Spoon and Mason Mintz stories. However, none of the eleven middle-grade books has a "buddy" theme. The three Magic Moscow books include a friendship between Norman Bleistift and his employer, Steve Nickelson, but Steve is understood to be considerably older than Norman and is more an adult mentor than a peer. Counting Steve Nickelson as an adult, we can say that all of the intermediate books focus upon a lone child interacting with adults . . . and giant chickens . . . and talking lizards . . . but not with other youngsters.

Thus far, we have been considering how Daniel Pinkwater's young adult books fit within his own overall body of work, and in what respects these half-dozen works resemble or differ from his own fiction for pre-adolescents and children. We must also ask where Pinkwater's books stand in the wider world of literature, and of contemporary young adult fiction in particular. In a recent article, Patty Campbell characterized the young adult novel in this way:

> The central theme of most YA fiction is becoming an adult, finding the answer to the question, "Who am I and what am I going to do about it?" No matter what events are going on in the book, accomplishing that task is really what the book is about, and in the climactic moment the resolution of the external conflict is linked to a realization for the protagonist that moves toward shaping an adult identity.[17]

If we review Daniel Pinkwater's novels in that light, we find that *Alan Mendelsohn, the Boy from Mars* and *The Education of Robert Nifkin* correspond best to Campbell's definition. Both are relatively conventional narratives in the *bildungsroman*[18] tradition, in which the young protagonist has experiences that propel him toward adulthood. In each we identify with the narrator and hope for him to succeed. One reason why those two books are most in accord with Campbell's characterization of the YA novel is that they also happen to come closer than Pinkwater's other four young adult books to fitting the definition of being novels of any sort! The two Snarkout books are filled with comic adventures, and the two Dada Boys books are rich in satire, but none of the four could be said to center upon "the shaping of an adult identity," or upon character development generally. Neither Walter Galt nor Charles the Cat, narrators of the Snarkout and Dada Boys books, respectively, are "heroes" with whom we strongly identify. Character formation is subordinated to humor and social commentary. So what are those four books all about?

We can more promptly answer the question, "Are these books young adult literature?" than the questions, "Are they novels? And if so, what sort of novels?" The young adult label does fit, despite the unconventional character and plot development in these stories. Noting other characteristics of the genre, Campbell observes that "there is an edge of anger always just under the surface in most young adult fiction; risky subjects can be explored, and the tone can be spectacularly dark."[19] Those qualities are especially evident in *Young Adult Novel* and its sequel.

Most important, all of Pinkwater's young adult works feature teenage narrators and their friends, and the books are clearly written and marketed for adolescent readers. His protagonists live in ordinary neighborhoods, attend public schools, and are faced with a wide range of adolescent challenges, especially interactions with their peers, and with parents, teachers, and other authority figures. Some young adult topics, such as sports, dating, and popularity, are treated only ironically in Pinkwater's books, when mentioned at all. Nevertheless, these half dozen works are unquestionably young adult fiction, although perhaps they are not novels in the traditional sense. What then?

Certainly, Pinkwater's books contain strong elements of comedy. The comic novel is not one of the most prevalent forms. Whether written for the adult or YA audience, it is difficult to pull off. Patty Campbell has commented, "The ability to write humorous YA fiction, to turn the traumas of adolescence into laughter without trivializing them, is a rare talent. We should cherish every writer who has it."[20] Arthea Reed adds, "understanding the humor of adolescence can be difficult for writers of young adult realistic fiction."[21] Reed mentions both of Pinkwater's Snarkout novels in her discussion of YA humor, along with works by Judy Blume, Judith Clarke, Ellen Conford, M. E. Kerr, E. L. Konigsberg, Gordon Korman, and Jerry Spinelli, among others. Although Pinkwater tends less toward realism than those other authors, like them, Reed says, he reassures adolescents: "You can survive," "Life is not so serious," and "There are other kids who share your problems."[22] In *Reading for the Love of It*, Michelle Landsberg describes Pinkwater as "probably the most sophisticated and surrealistic of America's humorists for the young."[23]

All of Pinkwater's young adult fiction contains satire as well as comedy, and in both *Young Adult Novel* and *Dead End Dada*, satire is the dominant mode. Pinkwater's portraits of incompetent teachers, psychologists, and other authority figures go well beyond comedy into the realm of social criticism. There is a genuine bite to these portrayals, an edge of savage anger and moral indignation that cannot be contained within the concept of humor.[24] Good instances of satirical young adult fiction are rare. Reed notes, "Few authors have attempted to write pure satire for adolescents," and she identifies only a handful of examples, including Sue Townsend's *The Secret Diary of Adrian Mole, Aged 13$^{3/4}$*, and several works by Julian E. Thompson. Reed notes that satire, as well as comedy, can be combined with science fiction and fantasy. She cites George Orwell's *Animal Farm* as a mainstream classic that is often read by adolescents.[25]

Humor blended with science fiction and fantasy, of course, is a genre mix for which Pinkwater is renowned. The section of Reed's reference work devoted to "Humor in Science Fiction and Fantasy" begins by naming Pinkwater's *Lizard Music* and his *Alan Mendelsohn* as supreme examples of this special combination. "Many of Daniel Pinkwater's books for young adolescents are extraordinarily funny fantasy or science fiction adventures."[26] The mingling of humor with science fiction and fantasy adventure is the hallmark of Pinkwater's middle-grade fiction, and it has its place in some of his young adult books as well. Other works of humorous science fiction mentioned by Reed include Paula Danziger's *This Place Has No Atmosphere*, and a pair of books by Ernesto T. Bethancourt, *The Dog Days of Arthur Cane* and *Tune in Yesterday*.[27] Bruce Coville[28] and Douglas Adams also produce fiction in this mode. Although the former writes primarily for preadolescent audiences, and the latter mainly for adults, the works of both authors are appreciated by many young adult readers. Aficionados of special genres such as humorous science fiction will often cross age-based boundaries to find the kinds of books (and films) they enjoy.[29]

Pinkwater sometimes mixes in elements of the detective or mystery story as well. Both of the Snarkout books, with their mystery subplots and hilarious caricatures of Sherlock Holmes and Dr. Watson, feature an extraordinary mixture of the four modes we have discussed: comedy, satire, fantasy adventure, and mystery. Such a complex mingling of genres might seem to defy classification, but in fact, a literary concept broad enough to encompass prose works as exuberant as Pinkwater's has been identified.

The great critic Northrop Frye described a form he termed "Menippean satire," after the third-century BC Greek philosopher, Menippus. Neither tragedy, nor romance, nor exactly comedy, this is a distinct genre in which plot and character are secondary to the ebullient flow of an author's satirical vision.

> The Menippean satire deals less with people as such than with mental attitudes . . . [it] differs from the novel in its characterization, which is stylized rather than naturalistic, and presents people as mouth-

pieces of the ideas they represent. . . . Petronius, Apuleius, Rabelais, Swift, and Voltaire all use a loose-jointed narrative form often confused with romance. It differs from the romance, however . . . as it is not primarily concerned with the exploits of heroes, but relies on the free play of intellectual fancy and the kind of humorous observation that produces caricature . . . the intellectual structure built up from the story makes for violent dislocations in the customary logic of narrative, though the appearance of carelessness that results reflects only the carelessness of the reader or his tendency to judge by a novel-centered conception of fiction.[30]

Examples of Menippean satire in classic literature include Petronius' *Satyricon*, Voltaire's *Candide*, Swift's *Gulliver's Travels* and Lewis Carroll's *Alice in Wonderland*. Joseph Heller's *Catch-22* is a modern classic in this tradition, and we might cite Douglas Adams' *A Hitchhiker's Guide to the Galaxy* as a contemporary example by an author who is often compared with Daniel Pinkwater. As Frye noted, such works depart from "the customary logic of narrative," and present caricatures rather than realistic or heroic characters, in order to achieve an effect not possible within the conventions of the realistic novel. Frye's references to "the free play of intellectual fancy," and to "humorous observation that produces caricature" are aptly descriptive of many of Daniel Pinkwater's books, particularly the Snarkout and Dada Boys stories.

Pinkwater's books are often referred to—on their dust wrappers, and by reviewers—as "wild and wacky" or as "zany romps." Such remarks are entirely unsatisfactory. How plebeian! How embarrassingly unimaginative! No, no, that sort of description simply won't do. The author himself has made this point,[31] but the irksome practice persists. As devoted connoisseurs of the matchless works of Daniel Pinkwater, it is our duty to correct anyone so ignorant as to allude to any of the master's gifts to civilization as a "zany romp." We must educate these critics and publisher's hacks by informing them that Pinkwater's books are not zany or wacky. They are classically molded examplars of that venerable genre, the Menippean satire, as any educated person should recognize.

But, even if it is conceded that Pinkwater's longer works are more soundly constructed than has often been supposed, can he be taken seriously when the subject matter of his fiction is so often silly and juvenile? Patty Campbell once described Pinkwater's primary audience as "perpetual seventh grade boys,"[32] and Pinkwater himself acknowledges having been strongly influenced by goofball juvenile humor. In an essay reprinted from one of his radio commentaries, he describes his affection for *Mad* magazine from its very first issue in late 1952:

> It was irreverent. It was crude. The humor was overdone, high-energy, laugh-a-minute, nothing sacred. In later years, I would encounter other exponents of the pandaemonic[33] style: the Marx Brothers, "The Goon Show," Monty Python, and the book review section of *The New York Times*. I felt as though I had discovered a new planet. This comic was drawn and written just for me.

A bit further on, Pinkwater continues, "For better or worse, whatever sort of writer I am today has a lot to do with those vulgar masterpieces I devoured in the 'fifties.'"[34] A remarkable statement from the celebrated author of over seventy books. Clearly, this is an artist who does not take himself overly seriously, and has not let fame go to his head. His ready acknowledgement of his debt to such, as he says, "vulgar" influences, is charmingly unpretentious. But does it brand him as a trivial writer?

To begin to answer that question, let's take a closer look at the essay just quoted, "On First Looking into Kurtzman's Mad." From its title through to its final punch line, the essay parodies John Keats' 1816 poem, "On First Looking into Chapman's Homer." Pinkwater's essay begins, "Much have I travell'd in the realms of gold. And many goodly jokes and cartoons seen." Keats' poem opens with these lines:

> Much have I traveled in the realms of gold,
> And many goodly states and kingdoms seen;

Midway in the essay, Pinkwater writes, "Like stout Cortez with eagle eyes, I stared at the drawings of Bill Elder and Wally Wood." The final stanza of Keats' poem:

> Or like stout Cortez when with eagle eyes
> He stared at the Pacific, and all his men
> Looked at each other with a wild surmise
> Silent, upon a peak in Darien.[35]

But the best is saved for last. At the end of this fine essay on his memories of the early years of *Mad* magazine, Pinkwater tells us that a classmate named Kratzner who had borrowed young Daniel's complete run of the magazine's early color issues was discovered to have suddenly moved to Connecticut without returning those precious issues.

The final sentence of Pinkwater's essay: "It would be better for you, Kratzner, if you come forward of your own free will, instead of sitting silent, upon a peak in Darien."[36]

The subject matter of this essay is commonplace: nostalgia for a "wacky" magazine of the 1950s, mixed with some personal recollections of the author's childhood. But the essay is a jewel. Some readers will recall that P. G. Wodehouse frequently quoted this same Keats poem in his immortal Bertie Wooster and Jeeves comedies. If that was what gave Pinkwater the idea of using "On First Looking into Chapman's Homer," so much the better. Wodehouse (1881-1975), was, like Pinkwater, a superb humorist who has also been underestimated because he restricted himself to light subject matter. Pinkwater's homage to both Keats and Wodehouse is quite fitting, and if anything, deepens the literary resonance of his essay. The comparison of Harvey Kurtzman and his *Mad* magazine to Homer's *Iliad* and *Odyssey* is delicious. Pinkwater's final play upon the identical names of the isthmus of Panama and a city in Connecticut, ending the essay with the haunting last line of Keats' poem, demonstrates both a high degree of literary wit and an outstanding ear for the sound of the English language.[37]

Like most of the classical and popular culture references that fill Pinkwater's fiction and nonfiction writings, the allusions to Keats, Wodehouse, and geography in this essay are throwaways. Many of the audience will not catch all of the references, yet one's ability to enjoy this well-told reminiscence by an accomplished raconteur does not suffer from ignorance of the allusions. Pinkwater's achievements in this essay are even more impressive when one recalls that this was one of hundreds Pinkwater broadcast on the radio, without any expectation that it would ever be published.[38]

We have belabored this particular passage from one of Pinkwater's essays in order to give a sense of the sophistication of the author's intellectual playfulness. His fictional works are filled with verbal as well as pictorial homages and cultural allusions.[39] There can be little doubt that Pinkwater is a witty, sophisticated, and highly entertaining writer. But is he more than that?

An easy and chicken-hearted response is that it is too early to tell. Pinkwater's work has not yet had a chance to be measured against the test of time. Moreover, the author is still in the midst of an extremely productive career. Some of his future books may impress critics differently than any he has yet written.

Pinkwater himself has made some very perceptive remarks about the literary value of his work in the essay, "Talking to Kids," originally addressed to the Children's Book Council. He notes that there is "small

A" art and "big A" art. The former is merely entertaining. The latter is more likely to "change your mind"—not just in the sense of influencing you to change one of your opinions, but in the deeper sense of actually altering your whole mind. "Most of the time, I try to be a writer of books that are Art (with a big A). I don't know when I've done it, because it's a tricky, sneaky, hard-to-define sort of thing." Going on to describe the challenge of evaluating work by other authors, Pinkwater continued, "It's hard to tell what is big A art and what is small A art. For one thing, big A artists make small A art sometimes, and you never know when a small A artist will turn out something that is big A. I'm not sure it even matters."[40]

So with that sensible advice in mind, this critic will not try to label Daniel Pinkwater as a "big A artist" or a "small A artist." But Pinkwater has certainly written some big A books. A good number of his picture books are perfect little gems. To select one favorite from each decade, *Big Orange Splot* (1977), *Uncle Melvin* (1989), and *Author's Day* (1993), are each without question highly original and outstanding children's books. Many of Pinkwater's other picture books are of similar high quality, and with their subject matter being so varied, preferences are very much a matter of personal taste.[41]

Among the shorter intermediate stories, the poignant fable *Wingman* (1975)—one of Pinkwater's rare non-humorous works—has been described as one of the finest short novels of pre-adolescent fantasy.[42] It also brilliantly captures the central and ongoing American theme of the immigrant experience in a manner as timely now as when the book was first issued a quarter of a century ago.

Two hilarious pairs of novellas represent a different, but equally fine achievement in the long story or short novel genre. *Fat Men From Space* (1977) and its sequel, *Slaves of Spiegel* (1982) are both masterpieces of comic science fiction. *Young Adult Novel* (1982) and its sequel, *Dead End Dada* (1985) are superb short satirical works for older readers, and they are indeed "heroic" as well as unique contributions to young adult literature. The brilliance of those four comic novellas has not diminished a bit since they were written two decades ago. As one critic recently noted, "They are amazingly free of details which would date them, and remain very amusing, very bizarre, and very much worth reading."[43] Each of the four will leave most readers limp with helpless laughter.

We come at last to an assessment of the full-length novels. Although all of Pinkwater's novels are sprinkled with wonderful, laugh-out-loud scenes, it must be conceded that some of the young adult and expedition novels are uneven, and several lack completely satisfactory conclusions. *Alan Mendelsohn, Baconburg,* and the four expedition novels—*Lizard Music, Yobgorgle, The Worms of Kukumlima,* and *Borgel*—are all terrific books. Each contains many high moments, but also a few low ones. The latter often involve monologues that slow the action, digressions that grab a few laughs without advancing the story, or weak endings. In short, these books are splendid adventures in the Menippean satire mode, but they each present some weaknesses to that reader or critic judging them "by a novel-centered conception of fiction."[44]

For the reader who likes his novels "straight," *The Education of Robert Nifkin* may be the most pleasing of Pinkwater's longer works. *Nifkin* is a work of consistent, sustained excellence, marching smoothly from a catchy opening to a perfect ending with scarcely a misstep. We argued in chapter 6 that *The Snarkout Boys and the Avocado of Death* is an equally well-constructed novel; however, full appreciation of that fact hangs upon the discovery of its hidden pith. *Avocado* is this author's favorite Pinkwater novel—and fruit![45]

For those with a craving for the smaller, spicier delectables of the Pinkwater cornucopia, that blue Spiegelian garlic awarded to Steve and Norman for their fine representation of our own little planet at the Great Interplanetary Cooking (And Eating) Contest may be the ideal seasoning. Indeed, *Slaves of Spiegel* is relished by many gourmets as Pinkwater's supreme novella—and food feast.

Having thus stuck out his neck (and tastebuds) with those judgments, the author now recalls some skeptical comments about book criticism from Daniel Pinkwater himself, which directly followed his remarks about distinguishing "big A" from "small A" books:

> I want to warn everybody to be very mistrustful of people who claim to know which is which. They usually don't know anything. Sorry— but it's true. The people who have to do with books—picking them, publishing them, selling them and talking about them (and that includes me for today only)—have a way of treating everything like big A art and making sure it's small A art. They may mean well, but you can't trust them.[46]

Gulp! Another critic put in his place by that fine serving of classic Pinkwater philosophy: think for yourself! Educate yourself, form your own opinions, and don't let "experts" tell you what or when or how to think. No author-illustrator of books for young people has communicated that theme more consistently or more effectively than Daniel Pinkwater.

NOTES

1. Daniel Pinkwater, *Uncle Melvin* (New York: Macmillan, 1989).
2. Daniel Pinkwater, *The Wuggie Norple Story* (New York: Macmillan, 1980).
3. Daniel Pinkwater, *The Snarkout Boys and the Avocado of Death* (New York: Morrow, 1982).
4. Daniel Pinkwater, *Attila the Pun* (New York: Four Winds Press, 1981), 36.
5. *The (Sort of) Official Daniel Pinkwater Website, Talk to DP Forum, Archive*, 27 <*http://www.designfoundry.com/p-zone* > (3 June 2000).
6. "Pinkwater . . . is the tender-hearted champion of every harmless eccentric and hapless outsider in America. But that doesn't stop him from spoofing their nuttiness either." Michelle Landsberg, *Reading for the Love of It*. (New York: Prentice-Hall, 1986), 174.
7. *Something About the Author*, (Detroit: Gale Research Company) vol. 46, 183.
8. *Something About the Author*, vol. 46, 187.
9. The "painful cheese burns" suffered by victims of the rampaging Mitsubishi Medium-Range Pizza Chef in *Baconburg* are representative of the sort of injuries a Pinkwater character might have reason to fear.
10. Daniel Pinkwater, *The Education of Robert Nifkin*. (New York: Farrar, Strauss, Giroux, 1998), 5.
11. As discussed in chapter 4, the longest of Pinkwater's pre-adolescent novels, his "expedition novels," are comparable to the author's young adult novels in length, language, and complexity. However, they do not deal with adolescent characters and issues.
12. That is, if they include any sub-adult human characters. Many of Pinkwater's picture books concern adult humans rather than children (*Wizard Crystal*, *The Big Orange Splot*, *Phantom of the Lunch Wagon*), while others are populated only by animals (*Bear's Picture*, *Wolf Christmas*). None of the picture or middle-grade books feature human adolescents. However, Young Larry the polar bear acts out some classic adolescent behaviors in the four books in which he stars.
13. The comically extreme behavior of many of Pinkwater's adult characters achieves much of its effect by virtue of being described from the viewpoint of observant and impressionable youngsters. Eccentric adults who maintain their individuality, refusing to conform to society's conventions and to the prevailing ethos of shallow materialism are among Pinkwater's positive role models. Pompous teachers, psychologists, and bureaucrats display behaviors an adolescent might hope to avoid.
14. The title character of *Mush, a Dog From Space* could be regarded as the ultimate Pinkwater character, since she is both an animal and an extraterrestrial.
15. *The Snarkout Boys and the Avocado of Death* includes an alleged extraterrestrial plot, which is found to have natural causes.
16. The Snarkout novels include—among other fauna—a fake orangutan, a werewolf, a pet alligator, and a dancing chicken; but the first two are not real animals, and the latter two are not essential characters.

17. Patty Campbell, "Middle Muddle," *Horn Book* (Sept/Oct 2000): 485.

18. "The German word Bildungsroman means 'a novel of formation': that is, a novel depicting someone's growth from childhood to maturity." Jack Lynch, *Guide to Literary Terms* <http://www.english.upenn.edu/~jlynch/Terms/Temp/bildungsroman> (4 June 2000).

19. Campbell, "Middle Muddle," 486.

20. Patty Campbell, "Best Books Revisited," *Booklist* (1 June 1998): 1740.

21. Arthea J. S. Reed, *Reaching Adolescents: the Young Adult Book and the School.* (New York: Macmillan College Publishing Company, 1994), 53.

22. Reed, 54.

23. Landsberg, 71.

24. A satire is "a literary work in which irony, derision, or wit in any form is used to expose folly or wickedness." *Illustrated Heritage Dictionary and Information Book* (Boston: Houghton Mifflin, 1977).

25. Reed, 60.

26. Reed, 60.

27. Reed, 60.

28. Bruce Coville (1950-) is the author of books with such titles as *My Teacher Fried My Brains,* and *Aliens Ate My Homework.*

29. As for films, the recent success of *Men in Black* (1997) and *Galaxy Quest* (2000), confirms the continuing popularity of humorous and/or satirical science fiction products from Hollywood. Daniel Pinkwater's fiction has elements in common with many of the films of this genre. For example, *Young Frankenstein* (1974), *Little Shop of Horrors* (1960, 1986), *The Rocky Horror Picture Show* (1975), and numerous Tim Burton films, including *Beetlejuice* (1988), *Batman* (1989), and *Mars Attacks!* (1996) all feature a heady mix of over-the-top black humor, collisions between wildly disparate characters with funny names, chaotic action, jarring anachronisms, and nostalgia, much in the spirit of Daniel Pinkwater's stories. Most of the films of Mel Brooks, Terry Gilliam, and the Monty Python players have a similar comic flavor, although some use historical rather than science fiction settings.

30. Northrop Frye, *Anatomy of Criticism* (Princeton, N.J.: Princeton U. Press, 1957), 309-10.

31. "Pinkwater himself denies publishers' assertions that his books are 'zany romps.' 'I don't know when I've ever romped in my life,' he says. 'I'm not even sure I've seen romping done. I wouldn't know romping if it were displayed before me. I guess maybe when I was very small I used to romp, because I wore rompers.'" Jack Lechner, "Pinkwater Runs Deep," *Village Voice Literary Supplement* (March 1986): 18.

32. Patty Campbell, "YA and OP," *Horn Book* (Sept-Oct 1997): 543.

33. Pinkwater has deliberately spelled "pandaemonic" in the old-fashioned way to emphasize the etymology of the word. Elsewhere he has discussed the Greek origins of the compound, from the god Pan and the notion of daemonism. Daniel Pinkwater, *Hoboken Fish and Chicago Whistle.* (Princeton, N.J.: Xlibris, 1999), 68. Pandaemonium is also the capital of Hell in Milton's Paradise

Lost. *Oxford English Dictionary Online* <http://dictionary.oed.com> (5 September 2000).
34. *Hoboken Fish*, 76-77.
35. John Keats, "On Looking into Chapman's Homer." *The Poems of John Keats* (London: Longman, 1970), 60-62.
36. *Hoboken Fish*, 77.
37. Those who describe the pun as "the lowest form of humor" reveal their ignorance of the power and utility of wordplay in literature, as employed by Shakespeare, Joyce, Nabokov, and other masters. Some of Pinkwater's wordplay, as in this essay, is quite functional, and not at all an extraneous demonstration of wit.
38. Pinkwater recently observed that the heyday of books based on NPR radio commentaries seems to have passed. This is unfortunate for his fans, since Pinkwater's radio essays could fill several more books. *Talk to DP Forum, Archive*, 5 (7 August 1999).
39. See chapter 2 for a brief discussion of the visual jokes in Pinkwater's illustrated books.
40. *Hoboken Fish*, 168.
41. Several picture books we did not find space to discuss here (lest a book about Pinkwater's YA literature be dominated by a review of his voluminous children's fiction) are beloved favorites of many readers. *Magic Camera* (1973), *Pickle Creature* (1979) and *Tooth-Gnasher Superflash* (1981), all long out of print but available in some libraries, each have their devotees.
42. Landsberg, 67.
43. Marshall, Joan, *CM: Canadian Review of Materials* (27 February 1998) <http://www.umanitoba.ca/cm/vol4/no13/5novels.html>.
44. *Frye*, 310.
45. The edible product of *Persea americana*, although green and not particularly sweet, is derived from a tropical New World tree, and must therefore be classified a fruit not a vegetable—as Mr. Galt would be happy to elucidate if we were to allow him the opportunity.
46. *Hoboken Fish*, 169.

Selected Bibliography

Primary Works

Books

4 Fantastic Novels. New York: Aladdin Paperbacks, 2000. (reprints)
The Magic Pretzel. (Werewolf Club Series, no. 1) New York: Atheneum Books for the Young Reader, 2000; Aladdin, 2000.
Big Bob and the Halloween Potatoes. New York: Scholastic, 1999.
Big Bob and the Magic Valentine's Day Potato. New York: Scholastic, 1999; Turtleback, 2000.
Big Bob and the Winter Holiday Potato. New York: Scholastic, 1999.
Ice Cream Larry. New York: Marshall Cavendish, 1999.
Big Bob and the Thanksgiving Potato. New York: Scholastic, 1998.
Bongo Larry. New York: Marshall Cavendish, 1998.
The Education of Robert Nifkin. New York: Farrar, Strauss & Giroux, 1998.
Rainy Morning. New York: Atheneum, 1998.
Second Grade Ape. New York: Scholastic/Cartwheel Books, 1998; Turtleback, 1998.
Wolf Christmas. New York: Marshall Cavendish, 1998; Scholastic, 1999.
5 Novels. New York: Farrar, Strauss, Giroux, 1997. (reprints)
At the Hotel Larry. New York: Marshall Cavendish, 1997.
The Magic Goose. New York: Scholastic, 1997.
Young Larry. New York: Marshall Cavendish, 1997.
Goose Night. New York: Random House, 1996.
Wallpaper from Space. New York: Atheneum, 1996.
The Afterlife Diet. New York: Random House, 1995; XLibris, 1999.
Mush: A Dog From Space. New York: Atheneum, 1995; Macmillan, 1995; Scholastic, 1996.
Ned Feldman, Space Pirate. New York: Macmillan, 1994.
Author's Day. New York: Macmillan, 1993; Aladdin, 1997.
Spaceburger: A Kevin Spoon & Mason Mintz Story. New York: Macmillan, 1993.
The Phantom of The Lunch Wagon. New York: Macmillan, 1992.

Chicago Days, Hoboken Nights. Reading, Mass: Addison-Wesley, 1991; in *Hoboken Fish and Chicago Whistle*, XLibris, 1999.

Doodle Flute. New York: Macmillan, 1991.

Wempires. New York: Macmillan, 1991.

Borgel. New York, Macmillan, 1990; Aladdin, 1992; also in *4 Fantastic Novels*, Aladdin Paperbacks, 2000.

Fish Whistle: Commentaries, Uncommontaries, and Vulgar Excesses. Reading, Mass: Addison-Wesley, 1989; in *Hoboken Fish and Chicago Whistle*, XLibris, 1999.

Guys from Space. New York: Macmillan, 1989; Aladdin, 1992.

Uncle Melvin. New York: Macmillan, 1989.

Aunt Lulu. New York: Macmillan, 1988; Aladdin, 1991.

The Frankenbagel Monster. New York: Dutton, 1986.

The Moosepire. Boston: Little, Brown, 1986.

The Muffin Fiend. New York: Lothrop, Lee & Shepard, 1986; Bantam, 1987.

Jolly Roger, a Dog Of Hoboken. New York: Lothrop, Lee & Shepard, 1985.

Young Adults. New York: Tom Doherty Associates, 1985.

Devil in the Drain. New York: Dutton, 1984.

Ducks! Boston: Little, Brown, 1984.

The Snarkout Boys and the Baconburg Horror. New York: Lothrop, Lee & Shepard, 1984; also in *4 Fantastic Novels*, Aladdin Paperbacks, 2000.

I Was a Second Grade Werewolf. New York: Dutton, 1983; NAL, 1995.

Roger's Umbrella. New York: Dutton, 1982; Penguin Putnam, 1985.

Slaves of Spiegel: A Magic Moscow Story. New York: Four Winds Press, 1982; also in *5 Novels*, Farrar, Strauss, Giroux, 1997.

The Snarkout Boys and the Avocado of Death. New York: Morrow, 1982; also in *5 Novels*, Farrar, Strauss, Giroux, 1997.

Young Adult Novel. New York: Crowell, 1982; also in *Young Adults*, 1985; also in *5 Novels*, Farrar, Strauss, Giroux, 1997.

Attila the Pun: A Magic Moscow Story. New York: Four Winds Press, 1981; Aladdin, 1995.

Tooth-Gnasher Superflash. New York: Four Winds Press, 1981; Aladdin, 1990.

The Worms of Kukumlima. New York: Dutton, 1981; also in *4 Fantastic Novels*, New York: Aladdin Paperbacks, 2000.

Java Jack. New York: Crowell, 1980. With Luqman Keele.

The Magic Moscow. New York: Scholastic, 1980; Four Winds, 1980; Aladdin, 1993.

The Wuggie Norple Story. New York: Macmillan, 1980; Simon & Schuster, 1984; Aladdin, 1988.

Alan Mendelsohn, the Boy from Mars. New York: Dutton, 1979; also in *5 Novels*, Farrar, Strauss, Giroux, 1997.

Pickle Creature. New York: Four Winds Press, 1979.

Return of the Moose. New York: Dodd, Mead, 1979; also in *Blue Moose; and Return of the Moose*, Bullseye Books, 1993; Peter Smith, 1995.

Yobgorgle, Mystery Monster of Lake Ontario. New York: Houghton-Mifflin/Clarion Books, 1979; Bantam Books, 1981; also in *4 Fantastic Novels*, Aladdin Paperbacks, 2000.

The Last Guru. New York: Dodd, Mead, 1978; Bantam, 1980; also in *5 Novels*, Farrar, Strauss, Giroux, 1997.

The Big Orange Splot. New York: Hastings House, 1977; Scholastic, 1977.

The Blue Thing. Englewood Cliffs, N.J.: Prentice-Hall, 1977.

Fat Men from Space. New York: Dodd, Mead, 1977; Dell, 1980; Putnam, 1989.

The Hoboken Chicken Emergency. New York: Simon & Schuster Books for Young Readers, 1977; Atheneum, 1999; Aladdin Paperbacks, 1999.

Around Fred's Bed. Englewood Cliffs, N.J.: Prentice-Hall, 1976.

Lizard Music. New York: Dodd, Mead, 1976; Dell, 1978; Bantam, 1988, 1996; Putnam, 1989; Peter Smith, 1991; Turtleback, 1996.

SuperPuppy: How to Choose, Raise and Train the Best Possible Dog for You. New York: Clarion, 1976. With Jill Pinkwater.

The Blue Moose. New York: Dodd, Mead, 1975; Dell, 1976; also in *Blue Moose; and Return of the Moose*, Bullseye Books, 1993; Peter Smith, 1995.

Three Big Hogs. New York: The Seabury Press, 1975; Scholastic Book Services, 1975.

Wingman. New York: Dodd, Mead, 1975; Dell, 1979; Bantam, 1992.

Fat Elliot and the Gorilla. New York: Four Winds Press, 1974.

Magic Camera. New York: Dodd, Mead, 1974.

Wizard Crystal. New York: Dodd, Mead, 1973.

Bear's Picture. New York: Holt, Rinehart and Winston, 1972; Dutton, 1984.

The Terrible Roar. New York: Knopf, 1970.

Short Stories

"Journal of a Ghurka Physician," 272-278 in *The Game Is Afoot*, ed. Marvin Kaye. New York: St. Martin's Press, 1994, 272-278.

Note: Several of Pinkwater's short books have been anthologized in short story collections. These include:

Devil in the Drain, in *Devils and Demons*, ed. Marvin Kaye. New York: Doubleday, 1987.
Slaves of Spiegel, in *True Horror Stories*, ed. Terrance Dicks. New York: Sterling, 1997.
Wempires, in *The Year's Best Fantasy: Second Annual Collection*, ed. Ellen Datlow and Terri Windling. New York: St. Martin's Press, 1989.

Books Arranged by Category

Nonfiction

Chicago Days, Hoboken Nights. Reading, Mass: Addison-Wesley, 1991; also in *Hoboken Fish and Chicago Whistle*, XLibris, 1999.
Fish Whistle: Commentaries, Uncommontaries, and Vulgar Excesses. Reading, Mass: Addison-Wesley, 1989; also in *Hoboken Fish and Chicago Whistle*, XLibris, 1999.
Hoboken Fish and Chicago Whistle. Princeton, N.J.: Xlibris, 1999.
SuperPuppy: How to Choose, Raise and Train the Best Possible Dog for You. New York: Clarion, 1976. With Jill Pinkwater.

Adult Fiction

The Afterlife Diet. New York: Random House, 1995; XLibris, 1999.

Major Reprint Collections of Fiction

4 Fantastic Novels. New York: Aladdin Paperbacks, 2000.
5 Novels. New York: Farrar, Strauss, Giroux, 1997.

Young Adult Fiction

The Education of Robert Nifkin. New York: Farrar, Strauss & Giroux, 1998.

Young Adults. New York: T. Doherty Associates, 1985, 1991.

The Snarkout Boys and the Baconburg Horror. New York: Lothrop, Lee & Shepard, 1984; New American Library, 1985; also in *4 Fantastic Novels*, Aladdin Paperbacks, 2000.

The Snarkout Boys and the Avocado of Death. New York: Morrow, 1982; New American Library, 1983; also in *5 Novels*, Farrar, Strauss, Giroux, 1997.

Young Adult Novel. New York: Crowell, 1982; also in *Young Adults*, 1985; also in *5 Novels*, Farrar, Strauss, Giroux, 1997.

Alan Mendelsohn, the Boy from Mars. New York: Dutton, 1979; also in *5 Novels*, Farrar, Strauss, Giroux, 1997.

Middle Grade Fiction

Borgel. New York: Macmillan, 1990; Aladdin, 1992; also in *4 Fantastic Novels*, Aladdin Paperbacks, 2000.

Slaves of Spiegel: A Magic Moscow Story. New York: Four Winds Press, 1982; also in *5 Novels*, Farrar, Strauss, Giroux, 1997.

Attila the Pun: A Magic Moscow Story. New York: Four Winds Press, 1981; Aladdin, 1995.

The Worms of Kukumlima. New York: Dutton, 1981; also in *4 Fantastic Novels*, Aladdin Paperbacks, 2000.

Java Jack. New York: Crowell, 1980. With Luqman Keele.

The Magic Moscow. New York: Scholastic, 1980; Four Winds, 1980; Aladdin, 1993.

Yobgorgle, Mystery Monster of Lake Ontario. New York: Houghton-Mifflin/Clarion Books, 1979; Bantam Books, 1981; also in *4 Fantastic Novels*, Aladdin Paperbacks, 2000.

The Last Guru. New York: Dodd, Mead, 1978; Bantam, 1980; also in *5 Novels*, Farrar, Strauss, Giroux, 1997.

Fat Men from Space. New York: Dodd, Mead, 1977; Dell, 1980; Putnam, 1989.

The Hoboken Chicken Emergency. New York: Simon & Schuster Books for Young Readers, 1977; Atheneum, 1999; Aladdin Paperbacks, 1999.

Lizard Music. New York: Dodd, Mead, 1976; Dell, 1978; Bantam, 1988, 1996; Putnam, 1989; Peter Smith, 1991; Turtleback, 1996.

Wingman. New York: Dodd, Mead, 1975; Dell, 1979; Bantam, 1992.

Picture Books

The Magic Pretzel. (Werewolf Club Series, no. 1) New York: Atheneum Books for the Young Reader, 2000; Aladdin, 2000.

Big Bob and the Halloween Potatoes. New York: Scholastic, 1999.

Big Bob and the Magic Valentine's Day Potato. New York: Scholastic, 1999; Turtleback, 2000.

Big Bob and the Winter Holiday Potato. New York: Scholastic, 1999.

Ice Cream Larry. New York: Marshall Cavendish, 1999.

Big Bob and the Thanksgiving Potato. New York: Scholastic, 1998.

Bongo Larry. New York: Marshall Cavendish, 1998.

Rainy Morning. New York: Atheneum, 1998.

Second Grade Ape. New York: Scholastic/Cartwheel Books, 1998; Turtleback, 1998.

Wolf Christmas. New York: Marshall Cavendish, 1998; Scholastic, 1999.

At the Hotel Larry. New York: Marshall Cavendish, 1997.

The Magic Goose. New York: Scholastic, 1997.

Young Larry. New York: Marshall Cavendish, 1997.

Goose Night. New York: Random House, 1996.

Wallpaper from Space. New York: Atheneum, 1996.

Mush: A Dog From Space. New York: Atheneum, 1995; Scholastic, 1996.

Ned Feldman, Space Pirate. New York: Macmillan, 1994.

Author's Day. New York: Macmillan, 1993; Aladdin, 1997.

Spaceburger: A Kevin Spoon & Mason Mintz Story. New York: Macmillan, 1993.

The Phantom of The Lunch Wagon. New York: Macmillan, 1992.

Doodle Flute. New York: Macmillan, 1991.

Wempires. New York: Macmillan, 1991.

Guys from Space. New York: Macmillan, 1989; Aladdin, 1992.

Uncle Melvin. New York: Macmillan, 1989.

Aunt Lulu. New York: Macmillan, 1988; Aladdin, 1991.

The Frankenbagel Monster. New York: Dutton, 1986.

The Moosepire. Boston: Little, Brown, 1986.

The Muffin Fiend. New York: Lothrop, Lee & Shepard, 1986; Bantam, 1987.

Jolly Roger, a Dog Of Hoboken. New York: Lothrop, Lee & Shepard, 1985.

Devil in the Drain. New York: Dutton, 1984.

Ducks! Boston: Little, Brown, 1984.

I Was a Second Grade Werewolf. New York: Dutton, 1983; NAL, 1995.

Roger's Umbrella. New York: Dutton, 1982; Penguin Putnam, 1985.

Tooth-Gnasher Superflash. New York: Four Winds Press, 1981; Aladdin, 1990.

The Wuggie Norple Story. New York: Macmillan, 1980; Simon & Schuster, 1984; Aladdin, 1988.

Pickle Creature. New York: Four Winds Press, 1979.

Return of the Moose. New York: Dodd, Mead, 1979; also in *Blue Moose; and Return of the Moose*, Bullseye Books, 1993; Peter Smith, 1995.

The Big Orange Splot. New York: Hastings House, 1977; Scholastic, 1977.

The Blue Thing. Englewood Cliffs, N.J.: Prentice-Hall, 1977.

Around Fred's Bed. Englewood Cliffs, N.J.: Prentice-Hall, 1976.

The Blue Moose. New York: Dodd, Mead, 1975; Dell, 1976; Listening Library, 1981; also in *Blue Moose; and Return of the Moose*, Bullseye Books, 1993; Peter Smith, 1995.

Three Big Hogs. New York: The Seabury Press, 1975; Scholastic, 1975.

Fat Elliot and the Gorilla. New York: Four Winds Press, 1974.

Magic Camera. New York: Dodd, Mead, 1974.

Wizard Crystal. New York: Dodd, Mead, 1973.

Bear's Picture. New York: Holt, Rinehart and Winston, 1972; Dutton, 1984.

The Terrible Roar. New York: Knopf, 1970.

Secondary Sources

Reference books with entries on Daniel Pinkwater

Authors and Artists for Young Adults. Detroit: Gale Research, 1989. vol.1, 231-241.

Children's Literature Review. Detroit: Gale Research, 1982. vol. 4, 161-171.

Contemporary Authors. Detroit: Gale Research, 1978. vols. 29-32, First Revision, 529. (Daniel Pinkwater)
———. vol.106, 15. (Douglas Adams)

Contemporary Authors, New Revision Series. Farmington Hills, Mich: Gale, 2000. vol. 89, 327-331.

Contemporary Literary Criticism. Detroit: Gale, 1985. vol. 35, 317-319.

Kovacs, Deborah, and James Preller. *Meet the Authors and Illustrators, Volume 2 : 60 Creators of Favorite Children's Books Talk about Their Work*. New York: Scholastic, 1993.

Landsberg, Michele. *Reading For the Love of It*. New York: Prentice-Hall, 1986.

Lynn, Ruth Nadelman. *Fantasy Literature for Children and Young Adults, an Annotated Bibliography*. 4th ed. New Providence, N.J.: Bowker, 1995.

MacNee, Marie J. *Science Fiction, Fantasy and Horror Writers*. New York: UXL, 1995.

Major Authors and Illustrators for Children and Young Adults: A Selection of Sketches from "Something about the Author". Detroit: Gale Research, 1992. vol. 4, 1889-1892.

Reed, Arthea J.S. *Reaching Adolescents: The Young Adult Book and the School*. New York: Macmillan, 1994, 53.

Something about the Author. Farmington Hills, Mich: Gale, 2000. vol. 114, 156-164.

Something about the Author, Autobiography Series. Detroit: Gale Research, 1987, vol. 3, 221-226.

Twentieth Century Children's Writers, 3rd ed. Chicago: St. James Press, 1989, 781-2. Pinkwater sketch by Janice M. Alberghene.

Ward, Martha, et al. *Authors of Books for Young People*. 3rd ed. Metuchen, N.J.: Scarecrow, 1990.

Other books and parts of books cited

Dachy, Marc. *The Dada Movement, 1915-1923*. New York: Rizzoli, 1990.

Daumal, René. *Mount Analogue*. Boston: Shambhala, 1986. Translation and Introduction by Roger Shattuck.

Doyle, Robert P. *Banned Books 1999 Resource Guide*. Chicago: American Library Association, 1999.

Frye, Northrop. *Anatomy of Criticism*. Princeton: Princeton University Press, 1957.

Illustrated Heritage Dictionary and Information Book. Boston: Houghton Mifflin, 1977.

Keats, John. *The Poems of John Keats*. London: Longman, 1970.

Onada, Hiroo. *No Surrender: My Thirty-Year War*. Translated into-English by Charles S. Terry. Annapolis: Naval Institute Press, 1999.

Richter, Hans. *Dada: Art and Anti-Art*. New York: McGraw-Hill, 1965.

Rosenblatt, Kathleen Ferrick. *René Daumal: The Life and Work of a Mystic Guide*. Albany: SUNY Press, 1999.

Twain, Mark. *The Adventures of Huckleberry Finn*. New York: Random House, 1996.

Zelazny, Roger. "Auto da Fe." In *Dangerous Visions*, ed. Harlan Ellison. New York: Signet, 1967, 496-502.

Articles

Blackburn, Doug. "*All Things Considered* Personality Charms Airwaves, Kids' Imaginations." (Albany) *Times Union*, 29 November 29 1998): 4.

Campbell, Patty. "Best Books Revisited," *Booklist* (1 June 1998): 1740.

———. "Middle Muddle," *Horn Book* (July/Aug. 2000): 483-87.

———. "YA and OP." *Horn Book* (September-October 1997): 543.

———. "The Young Adult Perplex." *Wilson Library Bulletin* (March 1982): 532.

Maughan, Shannon. "The 'Crocodile' Files." *Publisher's Weekly* (29 November 1999): 41.

———. "Pinkwater Cruises to Contentville." *Publisher's Weekly* (29 May, 2000): 43.

———. "The Pinkwater Effect." *Publisher's Weekly* (25 January 1999): 30.

Websites devoted to Daniel Pinkwater

Chinwag Theater Website <http://www.chinwagtheater.org>.

The Hoboken Chicken Emergencyclopedia
<http://home.earthlink.net/~stoba/hoboken/index>.

The Official Pinkwater Page <http://www.pinkwater.com>.

The P-Zone: Aileron's Unofficial Pinkwater Website
<http://www.pinkwater.com/p-zone> {formerly *The (Sort of) Official Daniel Pinkwater Website*}.

Note: During the 1990s, *The (Sort of) Official Daniel Pinkwater Website* was the only authorized Pinkwater website. It was created and maintained by fans, and supported by Daniel Pinkwater in various ways, especially through his responses to email questions posted there, many of which are quoted in these pages. In late 2000, *The Official Pinkwater Page* was created, and *The (Sort of) Official*

Daniel Pinkwater Website relocated and renamed *The P-Zone: Aileron's Unofficial Pinkwater Website.*

Other Web Resources cited

Contentville < http://www.contentville.com>. (1 September 2000)
Crisp, Marty. "Borders Books a Best Seller, Bailey White." *Lancaster New Era* (PA), 21 April 1996. *NewsBank NewsFile Collection* <http://infoweb.newsbank.com> (22 July 2000).
Encyclopedia Britannica Online <http://britannica.com> (15 March 2000).
LaFarge, Paul. "Welcome to Planet Pinkwater." *Salon.com Magazine*, "Mothers Who Think" <http://www.salon.com/mwt/feature/2000/02/04/pinkwater> (4 February 2000).
Lynch, Jack. *Guide to Literary Terms.* <http://www.english. upenn.edu/~jlynch/Terms/Temp/bildungsroman> (4 June 2000).
Merriam-Webster's Encyclopedia of Literature, 1995, Literature Resource Center. Farmington Hills, Mich: Gale Group Online. GaleNet <http://www.galenet.com> (15 June 2000).
Oxford English Dictionary Online <http://dictionary.oed.com> (5 September 2000).
Pinkwater, Daniel. "Pinkwater in Fat City! Daniel Pinkwater Finds His Dream Car." <http://cartalk.cars.com/About/Pinkwater-Car>. (One of Pinkwater's periodic contributions to the *Car Talk* Website <http://cartalk.cars.com> (31 July 2000).
Wann, Marilyn. "Daniel Pinkwater and the Afterlife." *FAT!SO?* <http://www.fatso.com/interview.html> (11 March 1999).

Selected Book Reviews

Alan Mendelsohn, the Boy from Mars
Booklist (1 June 1979): 1493.
Childhood Education (January 1980): 169.
Haskell, Ann. "The Fantastic Mr. Pinkwater." *New York Times Book Review* (29 April 1979): 32.
Horn Book (August 1979): 416.
Kirkus Reviews (15 June 1979): 690.
Lary, Marilyn Searson. "Humor in Young Adult Literature." *Catholic Library World* (September 1983): 80.
Lechner, Jack. "Pinkwater Runs Deep." *Village Voice Literary Supplement* (March 1986): 18.
Manning, Patricia. *School Library Journal* (May 1979): 66.

Reading Teacher (October 1980): 52.

School Library Journal (May 1979): 36.

Sutherland, Zena. "New Titles for Children and Young People: *Alan Mendelsohn, the Boy from Mars.*" *Bulletin of the Center for Children's Books* (November 1979): 54.

The Education of Robert Nifkin

Bulletin for the Center for Children's Books (July/August 1998): 408.

Children's Book Review Service (May 1998): 120.

Horn Book (July/August 1998): 495.

Horn Book Guide (Jan-June 1998): 347.

Kirkus Reviews (15 April 1998): 585.

Mallon, Linda. "Summer Reading List Colored by Blush of Youth." *USA Today* (2 July 1998): D.5.

Publisher's Weekly (23 March 1998): 101.

Rohrlick, Paula. *Kliatt Young Adult Paperback Book Guide* (July 1998): 8.

Sigwald, John. *School Library Journal* (July 1998): 98.

Waldron, Ann. *Philadelphia Inquirer* (14 June 1998): Q6.

Zwirin, Stephanie. *Booklist* (1 June 1998): 1749.

5 Novels

Book Report (March 1998): 35.

Marshall, Joan. *CM: Canadian Review of Materials* (27 February 1998). <http://www.umanitoba.ca/cm/vol4/no13/5novels.html>.

Dirda, Michael. *Washington Post Book World* (7 September 1997): 11.

Publisher's Weekly (7 July 1994): 70.

The Snarkout Boys and the Avocado of Death

Andrews, Peter. *New York Times Book Review* (25 April 1982): 51.

Booklist (15 March 1982): 961.

Children's Book Review Service (April 1982): 90.

Davis, Joann. "Spring Is a Season of Plenty for Children's Author Daniel Pinkwater." *Publisher's Weekly* (7 May 1982): 53.

Kenny, Kevin. *Voice of Youth Advocates* (August 1982): 35.

Kirkus Reviews (1 March 1982): 50.

Kliatt Young Adult Paperback Book Guide (Spring 1983): 16.

Twichell, E.R. *Horn Book* (June 1982): 292.

Unsworth, Robert. *School Library Journal* (March 1982): 150.

The Snarkout Boys and the Baconburg Horror

Albert, Walter. *Fantasy Review* (January 1985): 48.
Booklist (1 September 1984): 70.
Churchill, Betsy. *Voice of Youth Advocates* (October 1985): 284.
Dirda, Michael. "The Chicken at the Edge of the Universe." *Washington Post Book World* (10 June 1984): 6.
Drake, Ross. "Picks & Pans." *People Weekly* (17 December 1984): 42.
Horn Book (September/October 1984): 594.
Kiplinger's Changing Times (December 1984): 71.
Kirkus Reviews (1 May 1984): 52.
Kliatt Young Adult Paperback Guide (Fall 1985): 26.
Madden, Susan B. *Voice of Youth Advocates* (August 1984): 144.
Piehler, Heide. *School Library Journal* (May 1984): 92.
Science Fiction Chronicle (October 1985): 44.

Young Adult Novel and *Young Adults*

Andrews, Peter. *New York Times Book Review* (25 April 1982): 51.
Booklist (1 April 1982): 1014.
Bulletin of the Center for Children's Books (July/August 1982): 213.
Children's Book Review Service (May 1982): 99.
Davis, Joann. "Spring Is a Season of Plenty for Children's Author Daniel Pinkwater." *Publisher's Weekly* (7 May 1982): 53.
Dirda, Michael. *Washington Post Book World* (1 December 1985): 11.
Horn Book (June 1982): 301.
Kirkus Reviews (1 March 1982): 50.
Kliatt Young Adult Paperback Guide (Winter 1986): 31.
Lechner, Jack. "Pinkwater Runs Deep." *Village Voice Literary Supplement* (March 1986): 18.
MacDonald, Sandy. *New Age* (June 1982): 70.
Madden, Susan B. *Voice of Youth Advocates* (June 1982): 36.
Marcus, Greil. "Real Life Rock: Greil Marcus' Top Ten." *Artforum International* (February 1992): 24.
Publisher's Weekly (5 March 1982): 71.
Unsworth, Robert. *School Library Journal* (May 1982): 74.
Waldron, Ann. *Philadelphia Inquirer* (21 March 1982): R4.

Index

About the Author

Walter Hogan is a librarian and associate professor at Eastern Michigan University. He has published articles on a variety of topics, including American art pottery, animal welfare, and library technology. He lives with his wife and four cats in Ann Arbor, Michigan, across the street from the school he attended as a child, and four blocks from his family home. He managed to earn three degrees from the University of Michigan by walking as much as a quarter of a mile to his classes on the main campus, even in rainy weather. He did much of his research for this book at the main branch of the Ann Arbor District Library, a few blocks from his house. His son Jeremy, now a medical student, appears headed for a productive and law-abiding career despite having been exposed by a reckless father to many of the subversive books of Daniel Pinkwater.